ROBERT PATTINSON

ROBERT PATTINSON

SARAH OLIVER

JOHN BLAKE

Published by John Blake Publishing Ltd,
3 Bramber Court, 2 Bramber Road,
London W14 9PB, England

www.johnblakepublishing.co.uk

First published in paperback in 2010

ISBN: 978 1 84454 954 2

British Library Cataloguing-in-Publication Data:

A catalogue record for this book is available from the British Library.

Design by www.envydesign.co.uk

Printed in Great Britain by CPI Bookmarque, Croydon, CR0 4TD

1 3 5 7 9 10 8 6 4 2

Papers used by John Blake Publishing are natural, recyclable products made from
wood grown in sustainable forests. The manufacturing processes conform to the
environmental regulations of the country of origin.

Every attempt has been made to contact the relevant copyright-holders, but some
were unobtainable. We would be grateful if the appropriate people could contact us.

Dedicated, with love, to my husband Jon
and my friends Emily and Ieva.

Introduction

The *Robert Pattinson A–Z* is jam-packed with everything you need to know about Robert. No other book goes into so much detail, or tells all the set secrets and what really happened on the night when Rob was kidnapped.

Sarah Oliver has written over 700 articles on Robert and knows more about him than any other journalist on the planet; her work on all things Rob has been viewed by over 10 million people. She has worked with *Twilight* fans across the world to produce the most up-to-date guide to everyone's favourite vampire.

This book will refer to Robert as 'Rob', as this is what his friends call him. You can read it from start to finish, or dip in and out of it, as you prefer.

A is for...

Accidents

You might think that being an actor would be a safe job, but Rob would disagree. During his relatively short acting life, he has had his fair share of accidents – he even hurt himself on his first day on the *Twilight* set when he went to pick up Kristen Stewart.

He confessed to MoviesOnline: 'I managed to pick up so many injuries whenever I tried the simplest of stunts. I went to pick up Krist and I almost ripped my hamstring. It's not even a stunt. She weighs, like, 50 pounds – I literally did one squat. And this was after three months of training.'

Rob isn't the first actor to become injured while filming. Shia LaBeouf managed to cut his eyelid with shrapnel when filming *Transformers: Revenge of the Fallen* and Sylvester Stallone broke his neck working on *The Expendables*. He had to have a very serious operation as surgeons inserted a metal plate into his neck. Yikes!

Luckily, Rob has never been seriously hurt and usually escapes with just a few bruises. The people around him aren't always so lucky, though. Kristen's *Twilight* stunt double struggled to walk for a month after Rob dropped her while filming the car-stop scene in *Twilight*.

Rob told MyParkMag: 'The scariest stunt was when I run and I put my hand out to stop this car which is racing towards me. I had practised it a bunch of times but the car is, like, coming at 30 miles per hour. And I was sick on the day of shooting. I had taken antibiotics and I was really dozy, and the car went off its tracks. So there I am, holding Kristen's stunt double and my timing was off because I wasn't feeling too good and the car, like, hit me in the face. Then I dropped her and I couldn't stop laughing.'

Eventually he gave up doing most of the stunts in *Twilight* and let his stunt double take over instead.

'I did quite a few of them, but I had a good stunt double as well – he's a professional free runner,' explained Rob to journalist Sheila Roberts. 'I can do something, and get injured and look like crap playing it, or he can do it and make it look really good, and no one notices the difference. After a while, I tried to do the Tom Cruise thing, but I eventually gave up.'

Rob was forced to hand over even more of his stunts in the other *Twilight Saga* movies to his stunt double because no one wanted to risk him getting seriously hurt. Timing is so important with all of the *Twilight Saga* films because Edward isn't supposed to age so, if Rob were to break something and hold up filming, this would wreck the release schedules. Also, Rob has been busy filming other movies in the short breaks between *Twilight* movies so he couldn't afford to be out of action for any length of time.

Although Rob liked doing some stunts in *Twilight*, he wasn't keen on the harness he had to use to do the treetop scenes so he was probably glad when his stunt double took his place. He told the *Twilight Lexicon*: 'Because you're balancing your entire weight on two straps, like in your crotch, and also being pulled at 35 MPH and pretending to run, which makes it chafe against everything, it was just really, really unpleasant. And to make it real, you really have to go into the most painful position. Like, if you try to do anything to ease the pain, it makes it look really fake, so it wasn't really fun.'

Sometimes the press make up accidents to sell magazines and Rob's spokesperson is forced to release statements to reassure *Twilight* fans that the star is okay.

THE TREETOP
SCENES WERE
DIFFICULT TO
PERFORM.

Back in March 2009, it was reported that a gust of wind tore a metal advertising sign from its post and it had hit Rob on the head while he filmed one of his *New Moon* scenes. This was a complete lie and there was no truth in the story at all. Rob's spokesperson soon set the record straight, but for a while fans were terrified that he had been seriously injured. Another time when fans

ROB ON THE SET OF *REMEMBER ME* – HE'S ONLY BEEN MADE UP TO LOOK INJURED!

were concerned for Rob was during the shooting of *Remember Me* in June 2009. He was seen with what looked to be a battered and bleeding face. Actually, this was all done with make-up as his character had to be in a big fight and get arrested. Phew!

Acting

When you watch a Robert Pattinson movie he looks so natural onscreen that it seems like he's been acting forever. He is so convincing in his roles that you might think that he had attended the best stage school in London to learn his craft, but this couldn't be further from the truth. Rob has never been to stage school and only decided to get into acting as a hobby when he was fifteen.

During an early interview, he broke the news to the *Daily Mail*: 'It's all a bit of a surprise, the acting and fame. I never did acting in school. My dad was in a restaurant and saw a bunch of pretty girls and decided to go up and ask where they had been. They said they went to this drama club, so he said we'd better go down too! It's the only time he's done something like that. We went down there and I began to work backstage. Then one day I was the only one left to play a leading role. That was the first acting I'd done and yet somehow I got an agent.'

Rob had never even considered becoming an actor when he was younger: he thought he'd end up playing the piano in a bar, drinking whisky. He never saw himself getting a nine-to-five office job either but instead wanted to be the old guy at the piano, playing music. Music was, and probably will always be, his big passion.

The drama club that the girls from the restaurant attended was called the Barnes Theatre Club. It was a professionally run studio theatre that had been providing the people of Barnes and West Molesey with great plays to go and watch for over thirty years. It was the perfect place for Rob to start his acting career.

Joining that drama club changed his life forever. Not only did he get his agent because they watched one of the performances and thought Rob had potential, but he also met his good friend Tom Sturridge during his time there. Rob and Tom often went up against each other for the same parts, but they remain good friends to this day. Both managed to secure small roles together in *Vanity Fair* and Tom has gone on to play 'Young' Carl in *The Boat That Rocked* (2009).

After playing Cedric Diggory in *Harry Potter*, Rob decided that he needed to learn how to act properly and so he moved out of his parents' home and into a rented flat in Soho with Tom. He knew that Tom would be a great flatmate and they could learn how to act together.

Rob's whole face lights up when he talks to journalists about those days in Soho when his acting career had only just started: 'It was so cool! You had to walk through a restaurant kitchen to get up to the roofs, but you could walk along all the roofs. I didn't do anything for a year, I just sat on the roof and played music — it was like the best time I ever had.'

Anna Kendrick

One of Rob's friends is Anna Kendrick, who plays Jessica in the *Twilight Saga* movies. She was born in Portland, Maine. Anna was actually very lucky to get the opportunity to act alongside Rob and become his friend — she had to leave her first audition because she was feeling poorly. She was subsequently invited to a later audition and went on to win the part of Jessica. The Jessica we see in *Twilight* is different to the one we read about in Stephenie Meyer's books because the *Twilight* screenwriter Melissa Rosenberg decided to combine Jessica Stanley and Lauren Mallory to make one character.

When Anna was asked in an interview with MTV if Rob and Kristen had changed at all, she replied: 'No, of course they're the same — yeah, of course. They're so level headed. They've handled it so, so gracefully. I really don't know [how I would've handled it]. I would have

ANNA KENDRICK

gone insane at this point! But they manage to be handling it in their stride.'

Rob really enjoys hanging out with Anna and, although he spends most of his time with the actors who play the members of the Cullen family and Kristen, he does hang out with Anna and the rest of the Team Human actors. One night out, he was photographed with his arm around Anna, pretending to lick her face. They were only messing around, but the media claimed something was going on between them and the photos soon appeared on hundreds of blogs and websites.

It must have been really embarrassing for Anna and Rob to have their personal photos plastered everywhere.

Ashley Greene

Rob wasn't the only actor to face a backlash from fans when the *Twilight* cast list was first announced. Some fans objected to Ashley Greene playing Alice but that didn't bother her too much because they only raised concerns about her being too tall and her hair too long – they didn't question her acting ability as they had with Rob.

Although Ashley is one of Rob's friends, the male actor she's closest to in *Twilight* is Kellan Lutz (Emmett) – she knew him before they were both cast.

ASHLEY WITH KELLAN LUTZ.

Because Kellan and Rob are close friends and Ashley and Kristen are also good mates, they often hang out together in Rob's hotel room. Ashley is really impressed with Rob's musical ability and has decided that she needs to learn to play an instrument, too – she is the only member of the Cullens unable to do so. If she decides to play the guitar or piano, Rob could offer to give her lessons. He seems very patient and understanding, so would make a great teacher.

Recently, Ashley gave *OK! Magazine* an insight into what the real Rob is like: 'He's not the most sociable. He's not one of those people who can go and talk to anyone. He's kind of a hermit and a little awkward. He got thrust into this limelight, but he's dealing with it. I think it'd be kind of difficult for anyone.'

Auditioning

Rob might not have been to stage school but this has never stopped him from shining at auditions. His looks and talent have always shone through, leaving casting directors desperate to snap him up.

Twilight director Catherine Hardwicke was over the moon when Rob stepped into her audition room. She had already seen thousands of pretty boys wanting to play Edward but none of them was suitable. Catherine needed a pale-skinned actor who could play the most handsome guy in the world but still have the acting ability to carry off the role: Rob was the perfect choice.

Rob was quite relaxed about auditioning in front of Catherine for the first time; instead, he was more concerned about having to do his read-through with Kristen.

He confessed to Syfy.com: 'I think she'd done about ten readings that day. I was kind of intimidated by what she was doing; I was stunned because it was so different from what I was expecting. And I guess it never really changed the whole way through, which kind of works, just in terms of the story, me having to be the powerful one but being intimidated by her. The relationship [was] built from that... We really weren't trying to act like we were in love with each other right from the beginning – it was more about trying to intimidate each other and showing how much we didn't care about the other person, which I guess worked. In a lot of ways, that's how long-lasting relationships work.'

ROB'S FINAL AUDITION

Rob had to prove to Catherine that he was the right actor to play Edward by kissing Kristen on her bed during his final audition. Kristen had already kissed the three other guys who had been short-listed for Edward and Rob was the last one. It went so well that Catherine had to tell them to tone it down because they were so passionate.

'It was funny. When I got into bed with Kristen I said, "I've only known you for an hour and we are in bed,"' Rob revealed to the *Daily Record*. 'I think I must have gone way over the top with it as well, because I remember looking up afterwards and Catherine Hardwicke had a look on her face as if to say, "What are you doing? You look like you're having a seizure!"'

Afterwards, Kristen told Catherine that Rob had to get the part – or else!

Kristen explained to a journalist from the *Philippine Daily Inquirer* why Rob had stood out from the rest of the actors wanting to play Edward: 'Rob came into the

ROB'S FINAL AUDITION WAS WITH KRISTEN ON CATHERINE'S BED.

audition looking sort of terrified, like a subdued fear and pained; the pain was just very evident in him. I am not saying it's in Rob, but he knew what to bring to that character. We didn't need the statuesque, model-types who come in and just pose. I couldn't see any of the other guys – they weren't even looking at me, it was like they were focusing on their lines – but Rob is very organic. He's in the moment and he lets it happen, which is brave. He's brave. He's a courageous actor.'

Catherine was thrilled to have found her perfect Edward and really enjoyed directing Rob and Kristen in *Twilight*. During filming she told *VHM*: 'I do feel lucky directing Kristen and Rob, because their faces are so beautiful. They're expressive. Their skin is just porcelain, and sometimes I am literally watching the monitor and I'm going, "Oh, I'm so excited!" just jumping up and down. But I don't say anything, because I want to keep them in the moment. Sometimes I feel like I'm getting gold here. And it is very exciting.'

And Catherine wasn't the first director to feel like they had struck gold when they discovered Rob. The director of *How to Be* (2008) had been searching for his leading man for a year and a half before finding him. Oliver Irving knew straight away that Rob could play the part of Art because he understood the character and fitted in with the other cast members so well.

Awards

Rob's acting career might have only just started but already he has picked up several awards. His mum had better get herself a trophy cabinet to keep them in because they won't all fit on the family mantelpiece and he can't take them with him on trips around the world to promote his movies!

In 2008 he won a Hollywood Film Award and the Best Actor Award at the Strasbourg International Film Festival. Then, in 2009 he picked up a total of seven awards. At the MTV Movie Awards he won three Awards: Best Kiss, Best Fight and Breakthrough Performance Male. At the Teen Choice Awards he went one better and won four: Choice Hottie Male, Choice Movie Actor Drama, Choice Movie Liplock and Choice Movie Rumble.

He won his first award of 2010 at the People's Choice Awards. Sadly, he wasn't there in person to pick up the Award for Best On-screen Team with Kristen and Taylor Lautner. If 2009 was a good year for Rob, 2010 looks to be even better – his award tally should easily make it into double figures.

Opposite: Rob looks happy with one of his MTV awards.

B is for...

Bad Mother's Handbook, The

After a movie called *The Haunted Airman* in 2006, the following year Rob did another film for TV – *The Bad Mother's Handbook*. It was also based on a book, this time written by Kate Long. Sadly, Rob didn't have the lead as the story concentrates on three women in the same family. When the teenage daughter falls pregnant and is dumped by her boyfriend, she struggles to talk to her mum and her grandmother (who has dementia). Luckily, her nerdy, oddball friend Daniel (played by Rob) can help her every step of the way.

One of the funniest scenes is when Charlie is giving birth and Daniel tries to help:

> Daniel: You know, medieval women… uh… used to chew willow twigs for the pain. Contains a natural aspirin, apparently.
> Charlie: [shouting] Are you completely barking?
> Daniel: Barking, mad as a dog.

This is a fantastic film, but not many people saw it the first time around. It's now available on DVD.

Barnes

Rob grew up in a semi-detached Victorian house with five bedrooms in Barnes, southwest London. Barnes is a small Thames-side village, which boasts its own cricket green, rugby club, bookshop, delis, boutiques and restaurants. It's an affluent area and has some very rich residents.

Barnes is also home to one of the most famous music studios in London. The Rolling Stones, Jimi Hendrix, Oasis and The Arctic Monkeys have all visited The Olympic Sound Studios to record tracks. One day, Rob might even get the opportunity to record his first solo album there.

Bedroom

Rob has been to so many different cities, in so many countries, to promote *Twilight, New Moon* and his other movies that he doesn't really have his own bedroom any more. He has spent months at a time filming in Spain, America, Canada and Italy, and, when promoting his movies, he spends one night in one country, the next night in another place, and so on.

It must be strange for him when he sleeps in his old bedroom back at his parents' house on one of his visits to London. Rob has actually spent so little time there that he admits it hasn't changed much since he was ten. It's the complete opposite of the room he slept in while filming *Twilight*, which Rob described as being disgusting, not very sanitary and like an animal's cage.

When *Twilight* became a massive hit worldwide, you might have thought that Rob's hotel room for *New Moon* would have been upgraded to the penthouse suite or something, but it wasn't. It didn't even have a window and was on the 30-something floor, so Rob had a long way to travel in the lift to get to Reception. Despite not having any windows, he didn't complain and set about making the place as homely as possible. He likes being quite messy, though, and even refused to let the maids clean his room.

For *Eclipse*, things changed: because security around

ROB'S BEDROOM IS SOMETIMES JUST HIS ON-SET TRAILER!

Rob had to be so tight, it's believed he was given his own floor of a hotel to share with Kristen. Rob has to spend a lot of time in the hotel, so it's nice that he has the freedom and space to move around and to invite other cast members to visit. It would have been unfair just to make him have one small room.

When Rob's friends are on their way over, he says he's not allowed to ring Reception and ask them to let his mates come up to his room just in case they are imposters. Quite literally, he has to go down and carry them up. It's quite funny to think of him trying to carry Kellan or Taylor up some stairs!

#

Bel Ami is a new film set to star Rob as a character that he describes as being 'totally amoral'. It's an adaptation of a short story by the popular 19th-century French author Guy de Maupassant. Filming takes place in early 2010 and it will be released sometime in 2011.

It's not yet known whether directors Declan Donnellan and Nick Ormerod will decide to move the morality tale about a man who manipulates his wealthy mistresses so he can rise to the top into a modern-day setting as the original was a period piece. It looks as if Rob might be kissing Uma Thurman, Christina Ricci and a whole host of other gorgeous actresses in the movie. Of course, they are a lot older than his usual leading ladies.

Best Friends

Rob has had the same group of mates for many years. He would much rather hang out with them than find celebrity friends. When he's busy filming, he spends his evenings hanging out with Kristen, Jackson Rathbone and the rest of the *Eclipse* cast or chilling out in his hotel room, playing the guitar.

Sometimes his friends arrange gigs in Vancouver so they can catch up with Rob and spend some time with him. It's down to him that they are all building successful musical careers. When Catherine Hardwicke decided to include two of Rob's songs on the *Twilight* soundtrack, she changed the lives of Marcus Foster, Bobby Long and Sam Bradley forever. Sam co-wrote 'Never Think' with Rob, while Marcus and Bobby penned the bonus track 'Let Me Sign'. Suddenly, songs that the friends had written for fun were attracting millions of fans worldwide.

Rob told Fandango: 'The song on the soundtrack, "Never Think" – my best friend who taught me how to play the guitar wrote the lyrics for it last year and I made it into a song, and the other one ["Let Me Sign"] – me and another guy wrote. They weren't meant for the movie, but Catherine heard them and put them in the cut and I didn't know they would be on the soundtrack. I had thought it would be quite cool to have it be a secret thing and not have my name in the credits, like a marketing gimmick. It was nice, and also helped my friends as well.'

Sadly, he didn't achieve his wish of appearing anonymously on the *Twilight* soundtrack credits because his popularity meant that fans mainly bought the CD to hear his songs. As soon as it was released on 4 November 2008 it became an instant hit and sold 165,000 copies in the first week of release alone. It went on to become Atlantic Records' best-selling soundtrack ever.

ROB HAS MADE TONS OF FRIENDS ON THE SET OF *TWILIGHT*.

Two years ago, Rob and his mates never imagined anything might come of their jamming sessions on the roof of his flat in Soho. Back then, they would hang out until five in the morning, watching films, eating pizza, drinking and making music together.

It's such a shame that none of their singing/song-writing talents was used on the *New Moon* soundtrack. Their fans hope they will be included on the *Eclipse* or *Breaking Dawn* soundtracks and that at least two songs will be sung by Rob.

All three of Rob's song-writing buddies are glad that he has become a big star. Bobby summed him up to *Celebuzz* by saying: 'This is the best person all of this could ever happen to. It would never affect Robert the wrong way – he's exactly as he always was. He's very down-to-earth and humble, just a normal lad.'

Billy Burke

Billy plays Charlie Swan in the *Twilight Saga* movies. He loves playing Bella's dad and, although his character isn't the biggest Edward Cullen fan, he himself thinks Rob is great. In fact, Billy believes he has a lot in common with Rob, even though he's 19 years older than him.

Billy told Film.com: 'We both come from the same

BILLY BURKE AS CHARLIE SWAN IN *NEW MOON*.

life mentality: don't take anything too seriously, do the best you can in your work and relax when you're not [working]. We had a few laughs, a couple of drinks. Good kid! He's got a few songs in the movie [*Twilight*] and I'm a musician myself, but Rob's musical ability really blew me away. He's gonna go far.'

There doesn't seem to be anyone among the cast or crew of the *Twilight Saga* movies who doesn't rate Rob as a person and as an actor. This is really rare because often big actors can get other people's backs up by behaving like they own the set and by making demands the whole time – Rob doesn't seem to be like that at all.

Birth

Not much is known about Rob's birth on 13 May 1986 in a private clinic close to Barnes, London. His thrilled parents, Richard and Clare, named him Robert Thomas Pattinson but it's unknown how much he weighed or what sort of baby he was.

Even though Rob is often thousands of miles away from his family, his parents try to visit him on set whenever they can. For his 23rd birthday they made the trip from London to Canada to celebrate with Rob and his *New Moon* friends in a Vancouver restaurant. For Christmas 2009, Rob travelled to Barnes for a traditional family Christmas – his mum and dad must have been so happy to have him back home with them, even if it wasn't for too long.

Bodyguards

When Rob was filming *Twilight* he didn't need to have any bodyguards because no one knew who he was. Then, when filming was taking place on *New Moon*, he had three bodyguards tailing him but he didn't really need them – it was only local fans and a few photographers from regional newspapers who hung around the set locations, eager to catch a glimpse of him.

ROB IS LED AWAY BY HIS
BODYGUARDS ON THE
STREETS OF NEW YORK.

In the evenings, he could relax and visit restaurants without being bothered too much either. For *Eclipse*, things went up a notch: there were fans from across the world and twenty or so paparazzi stalking his every move. He has had to completely change the way he does things and now spends most of his time under his bodyguard's umbrella or hiding in his trailer. Whenever he leaves a hotel or a TV studio today, his bodyguards have to form a ring around him and help him get through the crowds and into his car.

Some fans become frustrated when they see bodyguards surrounding Rob but they need to understand that they are just trying to protect him. A situation that seems harmless enough can soon escalate if people get overexcited and try to push their way to the front of a crowd. When *X-Factor* winner Leona Lewis was punched during a book signing in October 2009, many people realised that being a star can be dangerous and lead to unprovoked attacks. Thankfully, nothing like this has ever happened to Rob but he still needs to be extra-careful when he's out and about.

Breaking Dawn

Breaking Dawn is the last book in the *Twilight Saga* and marks the end of the road for Bella and Edward's love story when the final movie is released. Ever since it

ROB AND KRISTEN ARE GREAT AT DEPICTING THE PASSION BETWEEN EDWARD AND BELLA.

was announced shortly after *Twilight* became a box-office hit that the *New Moon* and *Eclipse* movies would be made, fans were desperate to know if *Breaking Dawn* would be given the green light. When Rob confirmed in a *New Moon* press conference that *Breaking Dawn* the movie was finally going to happen and would probably be filmed in the fall of 2010, fans got their answer. *Breaking Dawn* will be the most difficult and challenging of the *Twilight* books to be adapted for the big screen: it will probably be split into two movies as there's a lot to try to cram into one. However, it's going to be hard to stay true to the book and keep the movie suitable for young teens. The following scenes will prove particularly challenging:

THE WEDDING NIGHT AND MORE PASSION
In the book, Bella and Edward's wedding night isn't described in detail but we know they break the bed and Bella ends up all bruised. Their lovemaking becomes even more violent once Bella turns into a vampire. It would be very hard not to show their passionate scenes, but this might prove impossible if movie bosses want to keep the movie suitable for a young audience.

RENESMEE
It's going to be impossible for one child actress to portray the half-human/half-vampire child Renesmee

Carlie Cullen that we read about in Stephenie Meyer's book. The birth scene will be horrific and, because Renesmee grows up at super-speed, several child actresses will be needed to play her in virtually every scene. Most probably, the abilities she has when a toddler will have to be computer generated.

THE ENDING

The ending to *Breaking Dawn* is a little weak for a movie and so this may need to be changed, although millions of *Twilight* fans across the world could be upset in the process. In the book, Alice sees an epic battle between the Cullens and the Volturi, but this never happens. Instead, they talk about their differences and no blood is shed.

However the director and screenwriter decide to adapt *Breaking Dawn* for the big screen, no doubt it'll be a big success. When the final credits roll, this will be a bit traumatic for fans, though, as it will be the last time that they get to see Rob play Edward Cullen unless Stephenie Meyer decides to write a fifth book.

Break-ups

Rob claims that he has never dumped a girlfriend and that it's always the girl who gets bored with him and tells him it's all over. In *New Moon*, it must have been

EDWARD BREAKS UP WITH
BELLA IN THE FOREST.

strange for him to have to finish with Kristen Stewart, even if it was his character Edward who was doing the dumping.

When Rob was asked in one interview with *OK! Magazine* what it was like to film the break-up scene between Edward and Bella, he replied: 'There's something weird about it. One of the main things I felt doing that, and what really helped, was people's anticipation of the movie and the fans of the series' idea about what Bella and Edward's relationship is, and what it represents to them. It's some kind of ideal for a relationship. And so, just playing a scene where you're breaking up the ideal relationship, I felt a lot of the weight behind that. Also, it took away a fear of melodrama. It felt seismic, even when we were doing it. It was very much like the stepping out into the sunlight scene at the end. You could really feel the audience watching as you're doing it – it was a strange one to do.'

Although Rob always insists he is single and that he isn't dating Kristen, *Twilight* fans still believe they are and hope their relationship lasts. They think it would be awful if Rob and Kristen went their separate ways before *Breaking Dawn* was finished because they might struggle to connect in the same way onscreen and this could ruin the final movie in the *Twilight Saga*.

Bryce Dallas Howard

On 29 July 2009, it was announced that Bryce Dallas Howard would take over the part of Victoria for the *Eclipse* movie. *Twilight* fans worldwide couldn't believe that Rachelle Lefèvre was given the sack only weeks before the cast were due back in Vancouver to shoot *Eclipse*. At the time, many of them said that Rob should go to the studio bosses and force them to change their minds. Instead, he welcomed Bryce into the cast – after all, it wasn't her fault that Rachelle had been dropped.

Bryce thoroughly enjoyed filming her *Eclipse* scenes with Rob and, when a journalist from *New York* magazine asked her about her co-star's personal hygiene, she defended him. In the past, numerous publications have suggested that Rob smells and doesn't wash. Bryce said: 'Actually, he's incredibly hygienic. He told me this story that made me crack up. He was like, "Oh, I have to go to the dentist." And I was like, "Oh no, what happened? Just a check-up?" And he was like, "No, I chipped a tooth." And I was like, "How?" And he was like, "Flossing." Who does that? I don't even floss. So he's hygienic, trust me.'

Bullying

Rob might be Mr Popular now but life hasn't always been easy for him. When he was younger he was bullied at school, but he refused to let the bullies win. One day someone stole the shoelaces from his shoes, but he just carried on wearing them and they became his trademark.

Indirectly, Rob has also helped victims of bullying who struggle with low self-esteem as thousands of fans claim watching him in *Twilight* has made them realise that it's okay to be a bit different and not fit in. In the future, it would be great if Rob could become the patron of a charity that clamps down on bullying – he is proof that you should never listen to bullies putting you down.

Opposite: BRYCE DALLAS HOWARD

C is for...

Cam Gigandet

Cam Gigandet plays James in *Twilight*. Despite their characters being archenemies, Rob and Cam got on really well during filming and on the promotional tour that followed. In fact, Rob has actually admitted that he would have liked to have played James if he hadn't been picked for Edward. His fans must be so glad this didn't happen – they would have been forced to say good-bye to him at the end of *Twilight*, when the Cullens kill James.

Although Cam must have been gutted to discover his character was to be killed off and that he wouldn't be

CAM IN CHARACTER AS JAMES.

CATHERINE HARDWICKE, THE DIRECTOR OF *TWILIGHT*.

joining Rob and the rest of the cast in Vancouver to film *New Moon*, we don't think he would have minded too much as his daughter, Everleigh Rae, was born on 14 April 2009. Not being in *New Moon* meant that he could spend a lot more time with the new baby.

Catherine Hardwicke

Catherine Hardwicke was the director of *Twilight* and, in many ways, the success of the movie is down to her. Fans might credit Rob and Stephenie Meyer with making *Twilight* a hit, but if Catherine hadn't objected to the first script she was given then a very different *Twilight* would have been made. The original version had been worked on so much that it hardly resembled the story in Stephenie's book.

Catherine divulged to *Time* magazine: 'Bella was a track star. Then there were FBI agents – the vampires would migrate south into Mexico every year, and FBI agents in Utah were tracking them. They ended up on an island, chasing everyone around on jet skis.'

And so the director turned away from the script, deciding instead to read the books. Instantly, she fell in love with the *Twilight* story. She then contacted talented screenwriter Melissa Rosenberg, the two ditched the first script and, together, they set about creating another from scratch.

Fans of Rob in particular have a lot to thank Catherine for because she was the one who went to the bosses at Summit and sold Rob to them. It was a hard job because he was relatively unknown, a lot heavier then and his hair was still dyed black from playing Salvador Dalí in *Little Ashes* (2008). Back then, he didn't look like the most handsome guy in the world, but Catherine knew that, with a bit of work, he could be just that. *Twilight* fans are so grateful that she fought for Rob to play Edward – they believe no other actor could have captured the essence of Edward so well.

Originally, both Catherine and Stephenie Meyer were keen for Catherine to direct *New Moon*, but they had to wait and see how *Twilight* did at the box office. When it was announced that *New Moon* was to be made, fans assumed Catherine would be at the helm – but they were wrong.

In fact, Catherine was offered the opportunity to direct *New Moon*, but she turned the job down. Although she knew that she had already gained a strong connection with *Twilight* fans, the actors themselves and author Stephenie Meyer, she didn't think that she could make a good movie in the given time. The film had to be ready for release in November 2009. She told EW.com that, despite being offered 'more money than [she] or anyone in [her] family had ever seen' for the second *Twilight* movie, she decided to say no and give someone else the opportunity.

Even though she has moved on to other projects, Catherine has maintained a great friendship with Rob, Kristen, Taylor and the rest of the *Twilight* cast. She hopes to get the opportunity to work with them again someday.

During the *New Moon* promotional tour, Rob and Kristen were photographed holding hands at a Paris airport on their way to London. The media went crazy and insisted the photos proved they must be dating. At the same time, an interview given by Catherine to *Time* magazine was released in which she discussed whether Rob and Kristen had been dating while filming *Twilight*.

Catherine admitted to *Time*: 'I didn't have a camera in the hotel room. I cannot say. In terms of what Kristen told me directly, it didn't happen on the first movie. Nothing crossed the line while on the first film.

'I think it took a long time for Kristen to realise, "Okay, I've got to give this a go and really try to be with this person."'

She also revealed that, after casting Rob in the role as Edward, she warned him not to start a relationship with Kristen – the actress was just seventeen at the time.

To date, Catherine seems to be the only one willing to suggest Rob and Kristen are an item: there

Rob as Cedric Diggory.

has still been no official statement from the onscreen lovers themselves.

Cedric Diggory

Rob's first big role was playing Cedric Diggory in *Harry Potter and the Goblet of Fire* in 2005 when he was eighteen. Back then he had no idea that in a few years' time he was to appear in *Twilight* and would go on to become a bigger star than Daniel Radcliffe, Emma Watson and Rupert Grint combined.

When Rob started acting, he was still at school and so it was hard for him to make the transition to being a professional actor on a film set. What's more, the *Harry Potter* cast and crew is one of the largest out there with literally hundreds and hundreds of people working together. The character that he was to play wasn't the easiest, either — he was involved in the Triwizard Tournament, which meant all his scenes were action-packed.

While Rob really enjoyed playing Cedric, he found filming to be physically very demanding. Shooting his scenes in the maze was particularly hard-going because he was hit by the hedges, pulled around on ropes and had to run around and hit Daniel Radcliffe (who plays Harry) in take after take. He also had to learn to scuba dive and act at the same time. From day one, he felt under immense pressure because he has never had any formal training in acting and he confessed to the BBC: 'On *Harry Potter* I was so conscious of the fact that I didn't know what I was doing, I used to sit on the side of the set, throwing up.'

While Rob might have doubted his ability to play Cedric, director Mike Newell knew he was the right actor for the job. He told one reporter: 'Cedric exemplifies all that you would expect the Hogwarts' champion to be. Robert Pattinson was born to play the role – he's quintessentially English, with chiselled public-schoolboy good looks.'

True, Rob did have the perfect looks to play Cedric, but he didn't have the right body to play him from the outset. Almost immediately, he was instructed to work on his fitness levels because Cedric is supposed to be an ultra-fit seventeen-year-old. While he was being measured up for the swimming trunks that he needed for the merpeople task scenes, the costume designer suggested he might be better suited to playing a 'sissy poet'. Poor Rob! The next day, the assistant director told him that he was to have a personal training programme.

He has since admitted: 'It was run by one of the stunt team, who are the most absurdly fit guys in the world. I can't even do ten press-ups! I did about three weeks of that and, in the end, I think he got so bored of trying to force me to do it that he wrote it all down so that I could do it at home.'

Rob did try to train at home but he hurt a shoulder and so he was forced to stop working out. Despite this setback, he still managed to look super-fit in all his scenes and made the different challenges look easy.

The Times named Rob their 2005 British Star Of Tomorrow after the release of *Harry Potter and the Goblet of Fire*. What a great honour!

During filming, Rob had felt really intimidated by Ralph Fiennes (Voldemort) because he was such a big movie star. Years later, he was so shy that he pretended not to know him when he bumped into him.

In his defence, he says: 'I didn't really talk to Ralph Fiennes while I was doing *Harry Potter* and the only thing I did with him was when he stepped on my head. Then I went to this play and he was there. And this girl said, "You've worked with Ralph Fiennes, haven't you, Robert?" And I was like, "Well, no…" and Ralph said, "Yes, I stepped on your head." And that was the extent of our conversation.'

It's a shame that Rob's character was killed off at the end of *Harry Potter and the Goblet of Fire* because he added an extra something to the trio of Daniel, Emma and Rupert. At least we saw a brief flashback to Rob/Cedric in the next movie, *Harry Potter and the Order of the Phoenix* (2007).

HARD TO BELIEVE, BUT SOMETIMES ROB HAS TO USE CHEESY CHAT-UP LINES!

Chat-up Lines

Rob might not have to try very hard with girls any more but there was a time when he was forced to use chat-up lines to get them to talk to him. In fact, he was quite a shy teenager and so he must have struggled to approach girls at first.

His favourite chat-up line was 'Will you marry me? I don't want to mess around!' He's lost count of the number of girls that he has proposed to over the years, but Kristen Stewart is one of them. When she mentioned in an interview that Rob had asked to marry her on the *Twilight* set, Rob admitted that he couldn't remember this but he probably had!

Another chat-up line he liked to use when sitting down next to a girl was to tell them, 'I just got out of prison.' He loved to say this seriously and then see the look of terror in the girl's eyes. Rob is much more comfortable when girls approach him to suggest going out on a date. That way, he's not worried about getting blanked or being made to look like a fool.

When he was younger Rob liked crazy girls who played hard to get, but, as he's got older, he has become less fussy. While promoting *Twilight*, Rob confessed that he was a relationship kind of guy but he couldn't find a girl who wanted to go out with him.

It's always hard for actors to find love once they

CHRIS WEITZ DIRECTS KRISTEN IN A SCENE FROM *NEW MOON*.

become massive stars. Some girls just want to go out with someone rich and famous, so Rob has to make sure they want to date the real him, not just his bank balance. Many fans think the only girl who can understand how Rob must be feeling right now is Kristen and, because she knows him so well, he would never need to use a chat-up line on her; they could just take things slowly and not feel under any pressure.

Chris Weitz

Chris Weitz was the director given the challenge of making *New Moon* a bigger success than *Twilight*. When he was first approached to direct Rob and the rest of the cast, he had never read the books or watched the movie. He wrongly assumed that *Twilight* must be a film for girls but, once he had seen it for himself, he realised his mistake and that boys would enjoy it too.

Rob really enjoyed working with Chris on *New Moon*. He liked the way that the director was very calm and focused the whole time and he enjoyed reading the detailed syllabus that Chris gave each cast member shortly before filming started.

Rob told Rebecca Murray from About.com: 'I've never had that, from any director. It was 40 or 50 pages long, in addition to a bunch of letters and emails, trying to show that he was on the same page as us and was

Kristen, Taylor and Rob at Comic-Con.

completely with us, in making the film. And he didn't falter from that attitude throughout the whole movie. It probably sounds ridiculous how much praise he gets. I was just with him and his wife in Japan, and she was even kind of sick of it, but he is like a saint. He's one of the best people I've ever met, let alone directors. In a lot of ways, it shows in the movie. It's got a lot of heart, especially for a sequel in a franchise. He's just a great person to work with.'

Although Chris liked working with Taylor Lautner on *New Moon*, he enjoyed filming with Rob in Italy more because he thinks it's the most beautiful country in the world. Indeed, it's where he married his wife and he just knew the scenes there would be great if they could get them right.

Comic-Con

Rob first realised that he was famous and that *Twilight* was to be a massive film when he attended Comic-Con, back in 2008. Comic-Con is a comic-book convention that's held in San Diego, California, each year and also promotes fantasy novels, video games, movies and so on. Up until that point Rob and the rest of the *Twilight* cast and crew thought that their movie would be small and would just appeal to fans of Stephenie Meyer's series of books.

'I did this event called Comic-Con, which is for sort of sci-fi enthusiasts and people camped out for, like, three days to go to it and there was, like, seven, eight thousand people, and they just screamed and screamed and screamed the whole way through the press conference,' he told radio host Elvis Duran. 'I think I could have been anybody, they just screamed when the word *Twilight* came on.'

On his second visit to Comic-Con in 2009 the response was even greater. Some fans had camped for a week to get a ticket to the *New Moon* press conference and catch a glimpse of the first trailer before anyone else. They loved listening to Rob, Kristen and Taylor Lautner talk about the film and went crazy when they saw the clip of Rob without his shirt.

New Moon director Chris Weitz was also there to share the reasons why he decided to direct the movie. Rob is well known for giving witty answers in interviews and Chris Weitz also likes to joke around.

He told the audience: 'I've been stalking Rob Pattinson for the last ten years, so, when I got a chance to get within touching distance of him, I jumped at the opportunity… Actually, I think it's really an extraordinary cast who did the first film and I was very keen to work with them. Like most people of the male gender, I hadn't read *Twilight* before the film came up, but, once I read it, I realised that it dealt with all those deep emotions that everyone feels: first love and heartbreak and the ecstasy of reunion. Having been dumped so many times in my life, I felt that I could sympathise with Bella's character.'

Rob and Chris have a similar sense of humour so they tend to bounce off each other in interviews. They connect well not only socially, but also professionally. In fact, they enjoyed such a good relationship during the filming of *New Moon* that Chris allowed Rob to point out ways that some of the scenes might be improved. During one scene when Edward talks to Aro, Rob sensed it wasn't going right and so he stopped filming to discuss the matter with Chris.

As Chris explained to the *Los Angeles Times*: 'I promised the actors that, no matter what, we would have time to discuss every single line. There was a line that he felt was repetitive and Rob wasn't feeling where he was in the scene. We worked it out and came up with some alternative dialogue. I can work on the fly a bit because I'm a writer-director, which is helpful. I don't feel stuck or panicky when an actor is not down with a particular piece of dialogue.'

Comics

Rob might not be taking over from Tobey Maguire in the next *Spiderman* movie but he's about to become a comic-book hero. *Fame*, a new comic-book series, is coming out, and Rob is to be the star of one of the editions. Lady Gaga and Taylor Swift will also appear in cartoon form.

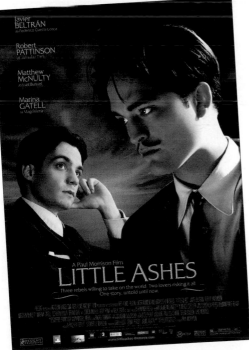

Above: Rob's first movie role was playing the older Rawdy Crawley in *Vanity Fair* (2004).

Left: The poster for *Little Ashes* (2008), in which Rob portrayed Salvador Dalí.

Above: Rob as Cedric Diggory in *Harry Potter and the Goblet of Fire* (2005).

Below: With Katie Leung, who played Cho Chang – Cedric Diggory's girlfriend.

Above: When *Twilight* came out, fans rushed out to try and catch a glimpse of Rob.

Below: His fans are some of the most passionate in Hollywood and always come out to show their support.

Rob and Kristen Stewart, who plays Bella in the *Twilight* movies, are rumoured to have a connection that is as strong off screen as on.

Kellan Lutz and Ashley Greene are great friends and hosted a Halloween party together in Las Vegas.

Stephenie Meyer, the author of *The Twilight Saga*, on the red carpet at the première of *New Moon*.

Bringing brooding, sexy vampire Edward Cullen to life on screen launched Rob's massive career.

The profile that
makes millions of
girls swoon.

D is for...

Daniel Radcliffe

In the last two years Rob has often been compared to *Harry Potter* actor Daniel Radcliffe. Each of them plays the male lead in their respective series and has a huge following. Although they are both successful, Rob has had to work a lot harder to get where he is now. Once Cedric Diggory was killed off in *Harry Potter and the Goblet of Fire*, interest in Rob dropped: he had to fight for parts in other movies and to convince people to hire him over better-known actors with bigger fan bases. Daniel Radcliffe, on the other hand, has been so busy

DANIEL AND ROB ACT TOGETHER IN *HARRY POTTER AND THE GOBLET OF FIRE*.

filming the remaining *Harry Potter* movies that he hasn't had the time or opportunity to appear in many other films. He has starred onstage in the West End and Broadway, though, when he played the lead in *Equus* from February 2007 to February 2009 and received rave reviews for his performance, which saw him strip naked for one scene.

Both Daniel and Rob are very honest and don't pretend to be best friends or anything. Daniel says they have only spoken about three words to each other since Rob left *Harry Potter*, but each of them wishes the other well. Daniel is hoping to catch up with Rob on the red carpet real soon.

Dating

Rob might have plenty of money now, but he didn't have much cash to splash when he was a teenager. He only earned a small amount of money from his paper round and a little from modelling assignments, so sometimes he couldn't afford to take his girlfriends on big, expensive dates.

Rob did take one girl on holiday, though, and he told *Bliss* all about it. He was doing a bit of modelling for the teen magazine in 2003 and they decided to run a whole page about him and the type of girls he liked.

Rob admitted: 'I once took a girl to Cornwall for the weekend. Mind you, we did stay in a dump and I forgot to mention that I'd been given the train tickets for free... but, hey, it's the thought that counts, right?'

He told them he loved girls who picked fights with him and his favourite chat-up line was 'Hi, you'll do [joke].'

Rob always likes to do interesting things on dates and isn't a fan of just going to the cinema because he tends to overanalyse films and point out their flaws. He took one girlfriend to the zoo but they couldn't afford the entrance fee and so they ran around the outside fence instead. It started to rain, but Rob thought this was romantic.

Despite these dates with unnamed girls, Rob insists he used to struggle to get anyone to date him. He

BELLA AND EDWARD ON A DATE.

revealed how it feels to suddenly become a sex symbol to the *Philippine Daily Inquirer*: 'It's strange because I'm a sex symbol to 14-year-old girls [laughs], which I guess is not the most helpful situation to be in. But yeah, I've never really thought of it; it's just so funny. I mean, just last year I couldn't even get a date [laughs] and then this year, the world turns and it's so bizarre [laughs] that everybody just changes their mind at the same time [laughs]. That's all I talked about the whole of last year: that I need to get a girlfriend. I need to get a girlfriend and then, this year, I could have any 12-year-old I wanted [laughs].'

Since becoming famous, Rob really hasn't been on many dates – he knows the paparazzi will follow them and that could put the girl under lots of pressure. He is still looking for his Miss Right but knows that he could meet her anywhere, even on the street or in a supermarket. He's a firm believer in love at first sight and would be thrilled to have the same kind of love as Bella and Edward.

Rob might be easygoing, but his sisters Lizzy and Victoria can be a bit overprotective at times. In the past, they've quizzed his female friends to check out their intentions. At the 2009 Cannes Film Festival, Rob admitted to z100 radio: 'I caught my sister saying to someone the other day, and she's a friend of mine as well, "Why do you like my brother? Like, is it just… do you like him because he's in movies?" And she's like, "You know what he is, he's just a really lying guy, he's a terrible person."'

We can't blame Rob's sisters for looking out for him – they just want to protect him. He has lots of female friends and so it must be hard for them to tell who wants to be his friend and who wants to date him.

'I have a very specific idea of how to be around women and stuff, but I mean I've never understood the point of hanging out with guys. What is the point?' he says.

David Slade

David Slade is the director of *Eclipse*, the third *Twilight* movie. Before taking on *Eclipse*, David filmed some pretty dark movies such as *30 Days of Night* and *Hard Candy*, and this influenced the way that he decided to tell the story. It's a lot darker and there's more action than in *Twilight* and *New Moon*. Although he wanted to stick closely to the original version in Stephenie Meyer's book, he preferred not to portray everything from Bella's point of view, either.

Charlie Bewley, who plays Demetri, told *OK! Magazine*: 'David is the master of mood, and the mood of *Eclipse* is very vicious and dark.'

Fans will be able to witness what vampires are really like at their worst in *Eclipse* rather than the sugar-coated

DAVID SLADE, DIRECTOR OF *ECLIPSE*, CARRYING A LOT OF AWARDS!

vampire activity we see in *Twilight* and *New Moon* when *Eclipse* is released on 9 July. Will Slade be able to make *Eclipse* the best of all the *Twilight Saga* movies? Only time will tell. We'll have to wait until the credits roll at the end of *Breaking Dawn* to be able to judge it against all the others.

Diaries

Rob loves to write and he likes to put together a character diary to help him prepare for roles. This allows him to really get in character and imagine what's going on in his character's mind. His fans hope that he will permit his diaries to be published one day so they can gain a deeper understanding of the process that Rob went through to play Edward Cullen, Cedric Diggory and Tyler Hawkins.

During the filming of *Harry Potter*, he carried a journal that he wrote in daily. He confessed to *Entertainment Weekly*: 'It was my diary but it became more and more and more about requests to the "fates" – "I will do this, if you provide me with this." It sounds absolutely ridiculous, but I had so much faith in this little book. I remember one time I wrote, "Please don't give me all my luck now. Make it all stretch – I don't mind waiting. Make it stretch for seventy years."'

But writing a diary alone wouldn't be enough for Rob

ROB LOOKING
THOUGHTFUL.

when it came to *Little Ashes*. Because he was playing a real person this time, he felt a greater responsibility to make sure that he portrayed Salvador Dalí correctly. This time he had to become the Spanish surrealist.

'I had this whole series of photos and I figured out the way he would move his body. There's a picture of him pointing. I spent days trying to figure it out, "How did he get his arm like that?"' Rob explained to MoviesOnline. 'It was the first time that I had ever got into characterisation, trying to work on movements. I was doing tons of stuff on his walk and such. It was probably unnecessary, but it was the one time I felt, like, slightly satisfied. But I wanted to bring that intensity to every job.'

Before filming for *Twilight* kicked off, Rob travelled to Portland three months in advance so that he could get a feel for the place and start to understand who Edward was, as well as the reasons behind his behaviour. With each new movie role, he seemed to spend more time in preparation than he had for the previous one. Always, he wanted to become a better actor and to develop his skills, too.

He told French magazine *15 à 20*: 'I don't know how it started [laughs] but I hadn't realised how difficult it was going to be to play Edward until I started reading the script. He's a very complex character. So I moved to Portland on my own, two or three months before filming began, and I didn't do anything but read the script and books to find anything that helped me play him. So I started to write things. I mean, if you really prepare for a role, there's going to be a moment in which he's all you can think of. So, I did things like little suicide notes. I was a little worrying, actually [bursts out laughing].'

It's just as well that Rob wrote Edward's suicide notes in Portland, not back home in London. His mum might have been worried had she seen them lying around his bedroom!

After *Twilight* came out on 19 November 2008, Rob sat down and watched it a few times and then started to make notes. He analysed his performance and noted what he felt he needed to work on in his next movie. Millions might have loved him in *Twilight*, but he knew that he could do better. Because Edward Cullen wasn't the central character in *New Moon*, Rob had more freedom to implement the changes he wanted to make. Even when *Breaking Dawn* comes out, we think Rob will sit down and work out what he might have done better – although there won't be another *Twilight* film. He's such a professional and so determined to become the best actor he can be.

Driving

Rob has never been one to say no to a challenge and even managed to learn how to drive on a ten-hour crash course. Despite not being a very good driver, he does hold an international licence, which allows him to do the required driving on the *Twilight* set.

Money and possessions don't mean much to him, so you won't see him in an expensive, flashy car any time soon. He still has the battered vehicle that he got when he first moved to LA. While filming *New Moon* and *Eclipse* in Vancouver, he was picked up from his hotel by a chauffeur, who drove him to the set each day in a car with blacked-out windows. This was to protect him from being chased by the paparazzi and it also allowed him to arrive at the secret locations without having to stress about where to go.

Quite often, Rob will ask his driver to pull over when he sees waiting groups of fans so that he can pose for photographs or sign autographs. Some fans spend all night in freezing conditions in the hope that Rob and the rest of the cast will stop and say hello. Rob always tells them they must be crazy to wait up, but thanks them for caring so much.

He thinks one of the biggest drawbacks to being famous is not being able to drive any more and admitted at the London press conference for *New Moon*: 'I miss driving. I never had a car in London, so I got one when I went to LA. But I've only had three months of driving [on my own] before I got started being followed by ten cars at once! Now I'm too scared to drive.'

If Rob wants to drive, he might have to put up with the paparazzi because they're going to follow him forever. If anything, he'll have more and more of them following him as his fan base grows and he makes even bigger films.

E is for...

Edward Cullen

Ask any *Twilight* fan who they love more, Rob or Edward, and they will probably struggle to answer. The Edward we read about in Stephenie Meyer's books and the one that we see onscreen make most girls dream of being Bella, but Robert Pattinson is equally handsome and charming in real life. In most cases, it's really impossible to choose between the two.

If you had asked Rob if he thought that he was in the same league as Edward before he was cast, he would probably have laughed out loud. Back then he didn't (and still doesn't) see himself as being 'the most

Edward Cullen

handsome man on the planet'. In fact, he really tried his hardest not to go to the audition because he didn't believe he stood a chance: only someone like Zac Efron would get the part, he thought, and so he didn't want to humiliate himself by even trying.

'The Edward in the book is like an enigma of everything that's perfect about a man. It's like, "He walked into a room and it hurts to see how beautiful he is." It's just kind of embarrassing. I just couldn't figure out a way to act perfect, I felt like an idiot going into the audition,' he confesses.

When he first auditioned, Rob knew little about *Twilight* and had no idea how big the series would become – he just wanted to try a different type of role. He divulged to journalist Rebecca Murray: 'I didn't want to do a stupid teen movie. I specifically hadn't done anything which anyone would see since *Harry Potter* because I wanted to teach myself how to act. I didn't want to be an idiot. This came kind of randomly and I didn't really know what it was when it first started. I was going to wait for another year. I wanted to do two or three more little things and then do something bigger. And then this kind of happened and I was like, "Well, okay…"'

Rob was actually on a bit of a high when he auditioned for the part of Edward because he'd not long finished filming *Little Ashes* and he'd had such an amazing time that the experience reignited his

ROB AS EDWARD.

passion for acting. Playing Salvador Dalí was so satisfying for him.

'I wanted to take that into *Twilight* and also try to break down the assumption that if a movie is being made from a book which is selling a lot of copies – which every single book that sells a lot of copies now is made into a movie immediately and they're virtually all not very good and everyone knows, even six-year-olds know, that it's just to make money – I didn't want to be involved in something like that.'

Even though we sometimes think of Rob and Edward as being the same person, he himself doesn't do that. Rob thinks Edward is a bit stiff and that he has a lot more fun. As he explained to *Twist Magazine*: 'Edward's this 108-year-old adult trapped inside a 17-year-old body, but I'm still a 6-year-old boy at heart... I look a bit like him.'

Playing Edward does have its downsides. Rob hated having to wear coloured contact lenses to get Edward's eyes right because it took him forty minutes to put them in and then they really irritated his eyes. He also feels that he's missing out because, unlike Victoria, Edward doesn't kill people. For Rob, the worst thing is the 'terminal groin-chafing from the harness' that he gets from doing the stunts.

Millions of girls might love Edward Cullen like he's a real person, but Rob thinks that's a little strange. 'If Edward was not a fictional character and you just met him in reality, you know, he's one of those guys who'd be like an axe murderer. He's ultra-polite and really formal all the time and like, "Let me open the door! Let me carry the bags!" Literally, you can just tell he'd freak out one day and shoot someone,' he pointed out to Dose.ca.

In order to play Edward, Rob read all of Stephenie Meyer's books to build a bigger picture of who his character really was. *New Moon* was particularly useful as it showed him how Edward should be played in *Twilight*. Many fans say that *New Moon* is their least favourite of all the *Twilight Saga* series, but for Rob it's the best book. He thinks the real Edward is revealed in *New Moon* rather than the idealistic one portrayed in *Twilight*.

Indeed, he told Film.com: 'In the second one, he [Edward] makes a mistake that's acknowledged by everybody, including himself. Also, he is totally undermined by more powerful creatures, and he's undermined emotionally by people as well. That's what humanised it. Since I read that book, I always liked him as a character, and I've tried to play that same feeling throughout the films. He's the hero of the story that just refuses to accept that he's the hero, and I think that's kind of admirable.'

Emilie de Ravin

The lucky actress who gets to kiss Rob in *Remember Me* is Emilie de Ravin. Her character, Ally Craig, dates Rob's character, Tyler Hawkins. Emilie is an Australian actress, who is best known for playing Claire Littleton in the *Lost* TV series.

In only a matter of weeks, Rob went straight from kissing Kristen in *New Moon* to kissing Emilie on the set of *Remember Me*. As soon as filming wrapped, he left New York and headed back to Vancouver to work on *Eclipse*.

Since Rob has become an international superstar, he hasn't been able to go on many dates, so, when fans spotted him with Emilie de Ravin, they were enthralled. The *Remember Me* lovers were hanging out in the Los Angeles County Museum of Art – dressed very sexily. Emilie was sporting a really trendy outfit while Rob was looking every inch the model in a designer suit. Some fans tried to get a closer look, but the rooms were cordoned off and security guards were placed at all the entrances. Later, it was revealed that, in fact, Rob and Emilie were doing a photo shoot for *Vogue* to promote *Remember Me*.

All of Rob's leading ladies seem to get on really well with him and Emilie is no exception. On 16 November 2009 she attended the *New Moon* première

EMILIE DE RAVIN AND ROB ON THE SET OF *REMEMBER ME*.

in Los Angeles to show her support even though Rob was really busy all night and couldn't spend much time with her. Her lovely, silvery-grey mini-dress made her stand out from the crowd.

During the TCA (Television Critics Association press tour) of January 2010, Emilie was asked to compare working with Rob with the male co-stars in *Lost*. She told the gathered journalists: 'Every experience with whoever you work with is always different. I had a great time working with him – we really made a point of working on our characters and their relationships and such. He's a really easygoing and nice guy to work with, which is always refreshing.'

Emma Watson

Emma Watson plays Hermione Granger in the *Harry Potter* movies. She's one of the most talented young actresses on the planet and Rob was thrilled to have the opportunity to work with her on *Harry Potter and the Goblet of Fire*.

When Rob first joined the *Harry Potter* cast, he was a bit intimidated by Emma, Daniel and Rupert. He knew they were all experienced actors and actresses and this made him feel a bit inadequate. To get over his nerves, he pretended that he was twenty-four and from South Africa and, instead of mixing with the other actors, he just sat

EMMA
WATSON

around drinking coffee for the first month. He soon dropped the act, though, and enjoyed getting to know Emma and the rest of the cast.

Rob and Emma are both hot property these days so they could well end up smooching in a movie in the future. They would make a great onscreen couple, even if nothing romantic happens between them in real life.

In the past, Emma has told the press: 'He's just a good friend! Girls love him [but] we're just friends – but he sure was great to work with.'

She's really glad Rob's acting career didn't come to an end after Cedric Diggory was killed off. And she's not the only one! Emma told *ET*: '[Rob] is a super nice guy. I'm really happy for him that he's gone on to be so über-successful. It's really good.'

Emma is currently taking a break from acting to study literature at the prestigious Brown University in the USA. In 2009 she became the new face for Burberry's advertising campaign and appeared in ads alongside her younger brother Alex who is a model. Maybe one day Rob could front an advertising campaign with his sister Lizzy.

Exercise

Rob's *Twilight* buddies Taylor Lautner and Kellan Lutz might like working out in the gym each day to make sure they look hot onscreen, but Rob can't think of anything worse. He hates exercising and prefers to be writing and playing music in his spare time. When he first landed the part of Edward, he was slightly overweight and so he was told to find himself a personal trainer and start getting fit, but he soon had to stop.

He told *Entertainment Weekly*: 'I used to go to the gym for about five hours a day but then I started losing so much weight. My head started to look really huge in comparison to the rest of my body. [Director Catherine Hardwicke] came up to me and said, "What are you doing to yourself?" To gain weight, I literally stopped exercising. Eating a cheeseburger after two-and-a-half months of doing that – it tasted like ambrosia.'

It's a good job his director noticed that Rob was exercising too much, otherwise he might have done himself some serious damage. It's always important to watch you don't overdo your workouts and that you consume enough calories each day.

When Rob is promoting his movies his schedule is so packed that he often has to eat on the hoof. He can't always choose what he wants, but has to eat what's available to hand. Also, he doesn't have much time to exercise during this time because he's constantly running from one interview to the next, but that keeps him pretty fit.

To make Rob look as if he had a six-pack during the fountain scene in *New Moon* without his having to up his exercise routine, the make-up artist painted on shadows so that his muscles appeared more defined. This was a lot less painful and time consuming than if he'd built up his chest in the gym. During the filming of that particular scene, Rob was really shy and kept ducking into the shadows every time Chris Weitz shouted 'Cut!' He didn't enjoy being half-naked, with hundreds of female extras watching his every move. In the end, Chris used a lorry to block out the extras' view so that Rob could just relax without feeling self-conscious.

F is for...

Fame

You would think that some of Rob's *New Moon* cast mates might be a little jealous of the fame that Rob has got through playing Edward. Although all the cast enjoyed a boost to their profiles after appearing in the first movie, only Rob was catapulted to the very top. Surprisingly, none of them is envious and, instead, many feel sorry for him because of the way that he's now followed everywhere.

His co-star Michael Welch (Mike in the movies) told MTV: 'Rob cannot be in public and be static for more than five seconds without being mobbed. If he's in a

ROB GETS A LOT OF LOVE FROM HIS FANS!

room and he looks down and he looks back up, [in that instant] everyone in the room will be staring at him. It's kind of ridiculous. [That level of fame] is literally Rob Pattinson and Barack Obama.'

Peter Facinelli plays Edward's dad, Carlisle. He shares Mike's concern for Rob and told the *Los Angeles Times*: 'I feel for Robert. He didn't sign up for this knowing what it would become. The fan base has grown ever since we filmed it. There were underground fans when we started. I remember we'd all go to their websites and they all said, "All these actors are wrong for the roles. Facinelli doesn't have blonde hair — what are they thinking?" For Rob, he just signed up thinking it'd be a cool little movie. All of a sudden he's like the James Dean of today. That's a lot [to] put on a guy's shoulders, but hopefully he'll be okay. He's kind of nerve-wracked; he doesn't leave his apartment a lot. But I think it'll be good — this will bring good things to him.'

It was probably only *Twilight* author Stephenie Meyer who had some idea of how famous Rob was to become right from the very beginning. She admitted shortly after he was cast: 'I apologised to Rob for ruining his life. There is going to be a group of girls who will follow his actions from now on. I asked the producer, "Is Rob ready for this? Have you guys prepped him? Is he ready to be the 'It Guy?'" I don't think he really is — I don't think he sees himself that way. And I think the transition is going to be a little rocky.'

Rob sees acting as a job and hasn't changed his lifestyle since becoming a superstar, even though photographers follow him and people wear his face on their T-shirts.

'I hope success hasn't really changed me at all. I mean, I don't feel like it has – I don't feel any different to what I did before. I guess my friends would have to judge me, but I don't feel any different,' he admits.

But the photographers who follow him are really sneaky and sometimes he doesn't know he's been snapped until the photos appear online and in magazines the next day. He told *Newsbeat Entertainment*: 'I think someone follows me. They do the most random stuff – I get a photo taken through a burger drive-through window and it's like, "What?" They always seem like they're six feet away. I don't understand. I'm walking around and I don't see anybody.'

Before *Twilight* came out, Rob was sent to media training to learn what answers he should give in interviews. In the end he decided to be himself and give honest, funny responses to questions. This could have been very damaging – journalists might have taken a dislike to him and printed negative stories about him – but that didn't happen and the press, like everyone else, fell in love with the real-life Edward Cullen. Rob has now given thousands of interviews, but no encounter is ever the same. He always thinks of something different to say and often drops in some golden nugget of information that his fans will love.

Recently, he has had to start saying no to interviews with some magazines because they keep printing stories that portray him as having a problem with alcohol. Rob knows they're doing this to try to sell more copies but he doesn't like being exploited or his fans getting the wrong idea about him.

He explained to the Australian newspaper the *Herald Sun*: 'Once you're becoming the "hot thing" or whatever, magazines say "Oh, we want to do a feature" and I've just started to say "No", because, as soon as you start putting yourself out there, people want to tear you down.'

THE PAPARAZZI CROWD AROUND ROB IN CANNES.

Rob has talked about the negative press to journalists based in the UK as well. He told Tom Shone from the *Sunday Telegraph*: 'In England if you want to look rough, you go out and get really drunk and come in looking really hungover but, if you do that in America, it's like, "Have you got a drinking problem?"'

Even *Twilight* director Catherine Hardwicke and *New Moon* director Chris Weitz have been hassled by fans wanting to get close to Rob. In fact, Catherine's own mother is a massive Rob fan.

The director told one interviewer, 'When I brought my seventy-year-old mother to the set, I asked her if she'd like to meet Rob and Kristen. To which Mum promptly replied: "Just Rob!"'

The level of fame that Rob has achieved in such a short time is truly remarkable. He might have to spend a lot of his spare time cooped up in a hotel now that he's so famous, but he tries not to let it get him down.

'If I'm still stuck in a hotel room in ten years' time and I haven't figured out another way to deal with it [fame], then I would be annoyed. I don't really think about [fame]. I just want to see what it's really like in two to three years,' he says.

Filming *Eclipse* was a lot more intense for him than *Twilight* or *New Moon*. He admitted to journalists on 11 November 2009 at the London press conference for *New Moon*: 'I was kind of trapped while filming *Eclipse*, but there's always ways and there's always places where you can disappear to – it just involves a bit more thought and you can't wander around willy-nilly.'

Family

Rob's family are immensely proud of him. They themselves have never been in show business and so they're finding it strange having to adjust to being the parents of one of the biggest stars on the planet. *New Moon* director Chris Weitz loved it when Richard and Clare Pattinson visited the set because they are so English and haven't quite grasped what a big star their son is. Even Rob admits that his parents don't understand why people ask him if he wants a cup of tea because they think he should get it for himself.

Both of Rob's parents are retired. His dad was a taxi driver and sold vintage cars when Rob was younger and his mum was a booker at a modelling agency. She helped Rob become a model but, when he 'stopped looking like a girl', the work dried up.

Rob has two sisters, Lizzy and Victoria, who are older than him and, as already mentioned, they can be a bit overprotective of him. Lizzy is three years older and Victoria is five years older than Rob. 'Up until I was twelve, my sisters used to dress me up as a girl and introduce me as "Claudia!"' he laughs.

Lizzy is a singer-songwriter and Victoria works in advertising. To begin with, Lizzy was the actor in the family and appeared in several plays before deciding to concentrate on her singing and dancing. She worked really hard and managed to get a Grade 8 in ballet then started singing in pubs and clubs around London. Lizzy was spotted when she was seventeen and asked to join the dance band Aurora. They released two singles, 'Dreaming' and 'The Day It Rained Forever', which made the Top Twenty, and went on tour all around the UK, Europe and North America. The band landed No. 1 on the Billboard Dance Charts when they collaborated with Milk&Sugar on 'Let The Sunshine In'. Lizzy was even involved in *Twilight* and sang background vocals for some of the scenes. Look closely at the credits and you will see her name.

Neither sister is at all jealous of Rob: instead, they try to support him in whatever ways they can. They don't want to become celebrities themselves by jumping on his success. Sometimes when they visit Rob in America, the paparazzi take photos of them leaving restaurants together and the next day their faces are plastered all over Internet sites, with people claiming to have found the *Twilight* star's secret girlfriend. That must be really embarrassing for the girls, but most probably Rob just laughs about it. He knows what the media can be like.

Rob was brought up in a smart area of London and

attended some very good schools. He told *The Inquirer*: 'My parents were just very aware of how you're treated differently in the world if you speak articulately, so it was just the way I was brought up.'

The real-life Edward Cullen has admitted in the past that his dog Patty is the member of his family that he is closest to. He can only visit the West Highland Terrier when he goes home to London to see his parents – which must be tough because he can't exactly ring up Patty for a chat!

When asked about his love life by myfoxphilly.com, Rob replied: 'My dog is the only lady friend in my life. I have a really girly dog, but she hasn't got a girly attitude. My dog is a little bit like Beyoncé – it has a Beyoncé walk, which is strange for a little terrier.'

It's a shame that Rob can't have a dog to keep him company in his hotel room but it wouldn't be fair on any pet. He works such long hours and travels all over the place that he would hardly have time to see it. Maybe in the future when he settles down and buys a home, he might consider acquiring Patty No. 2.

Rob loves dogs so much that, if he had to pick one animal to be, then it would be a dog. He disclosed to Gala.de: 'The lifestyle of a dog has always fascinated me. You sleep, sit around, get stroked, eat and get walked from time to time. That's great. There is a deep connection between me and dogs.'

Fan Mail

Some actors won't bother to read fan mail because they don't care all that much about their fans. But Rob is different: if you send him a letter, then he will read it and you might even get a signed photo back. Rob loves reading the letters he gets and unwrapping the thoughtful gifts fans send him. Because he's so popular and receives so many letters, it usually takes about six months to get a response, so don't be disheartened if you don't hear anything for a while.

'I go through it myself [fan mail], but I think I might get them censored, because I'm always expecting to get the one thing that says, "I know where you live and I'm going to kill you!" I'm always expecting that to come, but it never seems to arrive,' he told the *Los Angeles Times*. 'I never get any negative mail, so someone must be censoring them.

'I get a ton of letters. There was kind of a steady stream since *Harry Potter* but then as soon as [*Twilight*] came out... every week, there's like thousands more than there was before.'

And it's not just letters that Rob receives from fans. He's also sent cool gifts and books that his admirers think he will love. Rob always treasures everything that he gets because he knows his fans have spent a lot of time and energy picking out the perfect gift.

FAN MAIL STUFFED IN
THE HANDLE OF ROB'S CAR.

He told *Bliss*: 'I get sent some good stuff. I've gotten some really good books. I had this amazing thing made by a fan website, this really amazing bound book with all these notes inside it. I mean, it must have taken ages to make. I remember thinking, "Why?" But no, it was amazing. Someone sent me a book I'm reading right now, a book of Charles Baudelaire poems. I thought, "Wow, I was going to buy that!" That was nice.'

Rob loves that his fans stand up for him and won't let anyone print or say anything bad about him. He knows that, when a website features a bad story about him, thousands of his fans will leave comments underneath it and crash the offending site. It must help him, knowing people care about him so much.

If you want to write to Rob, here are the addresses you will need:

UK Address:
Robert Pattinson
c/o Curtis Brown Group Ltd.
Haymarket House, 5th Floor
28–29 Haymarket
London
SW1Y 4SP
England.

US Address:
Robert Pattinson
c/o Endeavor
Agency
Stephanie Ritz
9601 Wilshire Blvd.
Floor 3
Beverly Hills
CA 90210
USA.

Fan Parties

Instead of the usual film premières, *New Moon* held several fan parties around the world. There was one première in Los Angeles, but that was it. Rob found the London fan party the weirdest one of all because it was held in Battersea Park, not far from where he used to live. He spent less than twenty-four hours in London promoting *New Moon* before he had to jump on a plane for Madrid to promote the movie over there. Rob has admitted that it was really nice seeing his family and friends again, but so hard having to leave them virtually at once.

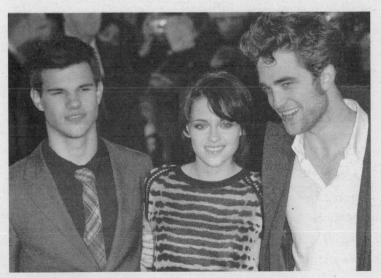

Taylor, Kristen and Rob attend the London fan party.

Fan Songs

Rob has some really talented fans that have written amazing songs for him. The best and most popular song is called 'She Wants To Be Mrs Robert Pattinson' and is by Welsh *Twilight* fan Sarah Barry Williams. Sarah actually wrote the song for her daughter Chariss.

The lyrics are so powerful that millions of Rob's fans can relate to them and the song has become an international hit:

She sits alone in her bedroom at night
Staring at his poster on the ceiling
And in her dreams and her fantasies
He knows her thoughts and her feelings.

She wears a T-shirt that says she loves him
So all the world can see
No other man could ever take his place
It's only Robert Pattinson she sees.

Chorus: She wants to be Mrs Robert Pattinson
Then all of her dreams would come true
Just to be Mrs Robert Pattinson
There's nothing she won't
There's nothing she won't do.

Her friends they think that it's a schoolgirl crush
On a star that's so far out of reach
But in her dreams in the twilight hours
Is where she and Mr Pattinson meet.

Like the stars that come out every night
And the sun that sets every day
In her dreams each and every night
They fly in the sky high above
They're flying away.

If you love Sarah's song, why not check it out on
YouTube or download it from iTunes.

Fans

Rob thinks that his fans are 100 per cent female, either
younger than twelve or older than thirty-five, but he
couldn't be more wrong. His fan base is made up of
both sexes, who can be any age. Rob's movies appeal to
all kinds of people from every sort of background.

Rob feels guilty when he doesn't have time to meet
his fans and thank them personally. 'You have to rush
through everything so much. I just feel terrible every
single time because people have queued up since 4
o'clock in the morning for five seconds, and that's it,' he
told CBS Channel 11.

He usually signs more autographs than the other *Twilight* stars because he always wants to make his fans happy. Sometimes his security team need to tell him several times that they have to go before he will listen.

During the *Twilight* promotional tour he admitted that he still finds it strange that, wherever he goes to promote series, he is always greeted by thousands of fans. He doesn't know why, but he's still shocked by people's reactions when he walks into a room or down a red carpet. Rob can be in virtually any city in the world and he's screamed at by mobs of girls. It always makes him feel really nervous and, in Italy, he burst into tears. He couldn't stop himself and he got really embarrassed when Kristen turned round and noticed he was crying.

Sometimes Rob wants to go around unnoticed and so he wears disguises. He likes to put on hats to hide his hair. Fans still seem to be able to recognise him, though. Rob finds the funniest encounters with fans are the ones he doesn't expect, like when old ladies in their nineties come up to him on the street to ask for his autograph. He finds it odd when they ask the same sort of questions as any twelve-year-old girl.

The weirdest encounters are when girls approach him with bleeding necks and ask him to bite them or when mothers request that he bites their babies. All this he finds extremely strange. He told *E! Online* about one incident with a seven-year-old fan: 'She went really

ROB SIGNING AN
AUTOGRAPH FOR A
YOUNG FAN.

quiet and she was like, "Can you bite me?" It wasn't a joke... I looked at her and thought, "Do you know what you're saying?"'

Fears

It's hard to think that celebrities have fears of their own. We imagine them being completely happy all of the time and not scared at all. But Rob isn't your average celebrity and he refuses to hide his fears from his fans.

In fact, Rob admits to being scared of quite a few things:

• Having his picture taken
• Seeing his face on posters
• Flying
• Darkness – he can't sleep without a light on
• Someone stabbing him
• Driving
• Crowds.

His biggest fear seems to be crowds and he explained to a journalist from *Girlfriend* magazine: 'I've been uncomfortable in crowds my whole life. I've always felt that everyone is looking at me [laughs]. So this doesn't make any difference. I could be in a supermarket and have a full-on panic attack when there's no one else there. And this was even like five years ago when nobody knew who I was!'

His fear of crowds might have become a bigger problem when he isolated himself shortly before filming for *Twilight* began. He told *Tu* magazine: 'In real life I've never been completely antisocial, although I was a bit when we were shooting in Portland and that comes with small disadvantages. If you don't speak to another person in a few weeks, you start feeling afraid of them, even when you order food at a restaurant. If I didn't go to pubs or bars, I would be running away in the middle of the night [laughs].'

Films

Rob is a massive movie fan and he's watched more films than most of us will ever see in our lifetime. He isn't your typical guy and into action or mainstream, but prefers to go for more artsy works instead.

IVANSXTC
Rob has watched the film *Ivansxtc* more than any other film. In fact, in 2008 he admitted that he'd seen it over 50 times in that one year alone. He must know all the lines by now! Rob believes that anyone who has watched the movie will know why he loves it so much. He really thinks Danny Huston is amazing in it and so

ROB SOMETIMES ADOPTS THE MYSTERIOUS LOOK.

he finds it a bit of a mystery that you can't buy the DVD in America, but it's no problem to get hold of it in the UK.

THE BEAT THAT MY HEART SKIPPED

Rob thinks that French actor Romain Duris puts in one of the best performances he's ever seen in *The Beat That My Heart Skipped*. He believes the gangster movie is the best modern picture he's watched in ages. Rob also likes another Romain Duris film, *Russian Dolls*. He loves the way that Duris is able to play characters that are the polar opposite of each other. In *The Beat That My Heart Skipped*, he is a tough gangster and in *Russian Dolls* he plays a bumbling novelist.

THE EXORCIST

We might think that *Twilight* is the most perfect film, but Rob would disagree. He believes *The Exorcist* is by far the most perfect and flawless picture. What's more, he doesn't think he will ever tire of watching it.

First Love

Everyone remembers their first love and Rob is no exception. He is always open in interviews and isn't afraid to admit that he was hurt by his first love but he refuses to name her. It's a good job because, if his fans ever found out who she was, then she'd be getting a lot of hate mail!

He shared with *Glamour* magazine: 'It's weird to enjoy your first love, especially if the relationship lasts a long time. Our relationship was really beautiful, but we didn't have an obsessive love [like in *Twilight*]. Her presence in my life made me very happy for three years. Now it's kind of hard to talk about it.'

Food

They say the way to a man's heart is through his stomach and this is certainly true of Rob. The *Twilight* star loves food, especially junk food. Because his mum lives thousands of miles away in London, she can't rustle him up healthy meals and so, when he's living in the USA or Canada, Rob usually eats pizza and burgers.

There are lots of good restaurants in Vancouver and so Rob ate out quite a lot with the rest of the *Twilight Saga* cast when they filmed *New Moon* and *Eclipse* in the city. Sometimes his 'dad' Peter Facinelli invited him round for homemade pasta, too.

Rob tries to sample traditional food in the countries he visits whenever he gets the chance. Attending his first Cannes Film Festival in 2009, he ate in the same restaurant as Brad Pitt and Angelina Jolie one night. He must have felt like pinching himself.

Sometimes Rob could do with his mum being around to keep an eye on him and see what he is eating and drinking. He confessed to *Seventeen*: 'I was just taking out my trash and I had, like, 300 cans of Diet Coke. It was just like, "How did that happen?" I don't even remember buying them. I also like Cinnamon Toast Crunch. My addictions are pretty much the only things I consume.'

Rob has bought himself his first microwave and is currently experimenting. He has been sticking all kinds of things in it – including a carrot!

Free Time

Rob has spent a lot of his free time making music with Kristen and the rest of the Cullens. He told one interviewer: 'Definitely on *Eclipse* as I was more confined to my hotel room. So I got a rented piano in there, in the room itself, which was really nice and I got a great guitar and, yeah, I've been trying to write some things. I haven't written any music in years so it was nice to start doing that again.'

When he's not making music, he likes listening to it and frequently goes to see live bands. He's a big supporter of Jackson Rathbone's band, 100 Monkeys, and can often be seen at their gigs. In August 2009, Rob and Kristen attended a Kings of Leon concert with other members of the *New Moon* cast. As Kristen and Rob leaned close together, a fan spotted them and took a picture of the two allegedly kissing. The next day, that photo was everywhere. On closer inspection, however, it seems to show them whispering something to each other, not kissing.

Future

Rob has never been sure what the future will bring him and so he always lives for the moment. After experiencing a level of fame when he played Cedric Diggory only to witness it disappear a few months later, he might be forgiven for thinking that, once all the *Twilight Saga* movies have been made, the same thing could happen again.

Asked in one interview how playing Edward Cullen has changed his career and where he wants to be in five years' time, Rob answered honestly. He said he didn't know because he had only done one other movie apart from the *Twilight Saga – Remember Me*, which was by the same studio. Rob feels slightly clueless as to his economic viability outside playing Edward. He's been offered parts in movies that he would never have been able even to audition for before, but still finds it all rather scary. He'd rather go through normal auditions than simply be given a part for being 'Robert Pattinson'.

ROB GETS HIS OWN HANDPRINT AT PLANET HOLLYWOOD.

'Before *Twilight*, I did any movie that I got and tried to make the best of it afterwards. Now, you're expected to come into the movie and provide not only economic viability, but a performance as well. People are like, "You can't just mess around: we're employing you to be a star and an actor." It's difficult and it's scary,' he admitted to About.com.

G is for...

Generosity

We don't know how much Rob has in the bank, but, after the success of *Twilight* and *New Moon*, it's likely to be a lot. After all, he has no big mansion or family of his own to support and he's so popular right now that he can't go on a shopping spree – he'd be mobbed by fans, plus he's never been one to care about wearing the latest designer clothes.

Rob likes to treat his friends when they visit him and he doesn't rub his wealth in their faces every two minutes. He has even shown his generous side when being interviewed by strangers: he told one interviewer from *Harper's Bazaar* to help himself to a pair of his sunglasses, saying: 'Do you want a pair? I've got 16!'

Girlfriends

It's hard to imagine, but Rob does have ex-girlfriends. Why anyone would want to break up with him or let him slip away is a mystery, though. In interviews, he refuses to name his exes and just says his heart has been damaged, but it's never been split in two.

Rob is such a nice guy that he's even helping out one ex-girlfriend. When Rob dated her she was a model, but now she's employed in a freezing works in New Zealand – she has to sort out boned-out meat when it comes down a conveyor belt. Rob has commissioned her to do a painting for him and she hopes that he will come and visit her once he has a week off from filming.

Some celebrities have to deal with ex-girlfriends revealing details of their relationship to newspapers. Rob doesn't think he has anything to worry about because he thinks his exes would struggle to remember him and he knows that his friends would never betray him either.

No one knows if Rob and Kristen Stewart are dating at the moment. They might be, or they might not. We'll just have to wait and see if they decide to spill the beans sometime soon.

In November 2008, Rob told the *National Enquirer* that he was single but a lot has changed since then. He said: 'I'm not dating anyone. I mean, I theoretically don't avoid it, but it's weird. I've been going to the same places every time I go to LA because they're the only places I know. And now everybody kind of knows me in those places. So, it's like I don't know. Just knowing that people will talk about stuff, and – you know. It's very uncomfortable. And also, if you try and chat people up, everyone's like, "Oh, he's such a – You're an actor: you probably go around sleeping with everybody." So, it kind of has the reverse effect of what you would have thought.'

Rob doesn't mind when newspapers and magazines report that he's dating various celebrities, even though this is not the case. He shared with a reporter from *Showbiz Spy*: 'I am single at the moment, but I read stories in the magazines and papers that I am dating so and so. But it's not true. But they are very good guesses because I always fancy the girl they pair me up with. I'm hoping it's the girl herself who has made it up – then I'm in with a real chance. Maybe I should start getting in touch with them!'

If you think you could be Rob's perfect woman, you might be interested to know what he looks for in a potential girlfriend. He likes girls that are a bit mad and are really strong personalities – but he often regrets finding such girls attractive.

EDWARD AND BELLA ARE THE PERFECT COUPLE.

H is for...

Hair

Rob finds it strange that people are obsessed with his hair because he hates washing it and just leaves it as he finds it when he wakes up each morning. He also thinks his hairstyle isn't all that unique – he knows lots of lads his age in London who have the same style.

We might notice when Rob runs his hands through his hair during video interviews but he does this subconsciously, so he doesn't always realise he's doing it. Some fans love his hair so much that they complain when he wears a hat. When he was doing one video interview in New York, people were allowed to text in messages and 95 per cent of them asked him to take his hat off. He was flabbergasted that people cared so much.

Rob thinks it's bizarre that his hair has become his trademark because he used to hate his dad brushing it when he was younger. He always jokes that he has a dandruff problem, but that doesn't seem to make girls find him any less attractive.

We might love Edward's spiky hairstyle in *Twilight*, but originally Catherine Hardwicke planned for Rob to wear a long wig. As she explains in her *Director's Notebook* which came out in March 2009: 'I thought he would look good with long, "timeless" hair, so Rob spent eight hours in the chair. Nicole Frank, assistant hairstylist, put in extensions. Rob *hated* them! The next day, Nicole yanked them out, and she and Mary Ann and Rob started working on the now-famous Edward hairstyle.'

In December 2008, Rob was fed up with all the attention his hair was getting and decided to have it cut. The crew-cut look didn't go down too well with many fans that feared he might look different in *New Moon* because of it. Luckily for them it grew really quickly and was back to Rob's normal long style before the cameras started to roll.

Rob's hair is always the centre of attention.

Haunted Airman, The

In 2006, the year after *Harry Potter and the Goblet of Fire* was released, things went very quiet for Rob. He only did one film and that was for TV. *The Haunted Airman* was based on the 1948 Dennis Wheatley novel *The Haunting of Toby Jugg*. Rob plays the main part of Toby – a pilot who returns home from war to be confined to a wheelchair (he is looked after by an aunt and a psychiatrist). It's a very dark movie and well worth watching to see another side to Rob.

He told one interviewer: 'My best acting experience was *The Haunted Airman* for BBC2. I play a World War Two pilot, who gets shot and paralysed. He gets terrible shellshock and basically goes insane. It's a great part. I was in a wheelchair all the time, which is always good, just chain-smoking throughout the entire film.'

How to Be

If you love Rob because of *Twilight* or *Harry Potter*, you might not be aware that he played the character of Art in a small film called *How to Be* (2008). If you haven't seen it, check it out – it's nice to see Rob in a different sort of role.

Art is a really odd, quirky guy, who feels miserable

most of the time. In an attempt to get his life back on track, he hires a self-help guru to come and live with him and his parents.

The director of the movie wanted Rob to look as ugly as possible, but nothing could make our favourite actor not look hot! He banned him from cutting his hair and gave him trousers that were too short. Making *How to Be* proved to be a turning point for Rob – he had actually considered giving up acting at the time.

He divulged to *IFC*: 'I really felt that I didn't know whether I wanted to be an actor. I didn't know what I was doing, I hadn't gone to university… you know, I was kind of bumming around and not feeling very good at anything but at the same time desperately wanting to be, but thinking that you'll never reach your own… the goals you set yourself.'

Ultimately, he found playing Art really interesting and it made him want to keep on acting. Of his character, he said: 'He's kind of, I guess you'd call him kind of a mediocrity – I mean, he doesn't really fit into any kind of people grouping. He's not particularly depressed, but he thinks he is. He doesn't have any kind of consistency in his emotions, which I think most people are like. Normally in films, if somebody's a sad person, they're a sad person but he's not particularly sad all the time – he's just basically chasing his tail. He's just a guy who is really stuck in a rut and he needs to figure a way out of it. I've never really felt stuck in anything. Art really feels like he's been trapped by his own life and he's kind of resentful about it as well. It would be really difficult to be friends with someone like Art. It seems like he's very real, but really he's a very demanding friend, he's very emotionally draining.'

Rob really stood out in the movie and was named Best Actor 2008 at the Strasbourg Film Festival. On the back of playing Art, Moviefone included him in its list of 'The Hottest Actors Under 25'.

Everyone involved with the film is so thankful Rob was cast as Art – not only did he do a good job but he also brought a huge audience to see the movie. They were able to release the film on DVD plus a soundtrack, too. This would never have been possible had *Twilight* not made Rob a massive star already.

Humour

Twilight author Stephenie Meyer revealed what the real Rob is like to Oprah Winfrey. She said: 'He smells great! Rob is hilarious, he is the funniest person – he's really fun to hang out with. He's not at all like the Edward character. It's interesting to kind of watch him shift back and forth because he's so different from Rob: he just changes, his whole face changes. It's amazing to watch.'

All of Rob's fans know that he has a great sense of

humour and it would be nice if he did a feel-good comedy movie one day.

Hygiene

Rob will never be a neat freak: he likes having a messy room and doesn't care about the way he looks. He hates having to change his clothes and admits there are times when he can't even stand his own smell.

Rob blames the fact that he is always travelling on not washing his clothes very often. He even nicked some of Edward's clothes to wear, but was embarrassed when an interviewer noticed! When he was playing Art in *How to Be*, the director asked him to bring some of his own clothes to add to his character's wardrobe, so in the end 50 per cent were his clothes and 50 per cent belonged to Art. After filming wrapped, Rob kept hold of some of Art's clothes to wear afterwards – which seems strange considering how awful they were. Some of the trousers were two inches too short in the leg.

He told Terri Seymour: 'It's, like, I don't clean my apartment 'cos I don't care. I have my apartment for sleeping in and I have my hair for just, you know, hanging out on my head. I don't care if it's clean or not.'

When he was shooting *Eclipse*, Rob let a journalist interview him in his hotel room and they spotted lots of boxes in a corner. When they asked him what was

ROB'S GOT A GREAT
SENSE OF HUMOUR.

inside, he revealed: 'Most of it is my dirty washing from New York. I didn't do any washing the whole time I was there – I just put it in boxes and shipped them up here.'

We don't think Rob's mum would be happy if she knew that he wasn't washing his clothes and was instead 'borrowing' socks and underwear from Edward's wardrobe!

Hype

Rob might have over 10 million fans and be one of the most talked-about stars on the planet, but he still keeps his feet on the ground. He doesn't want to follow in the footsteps of other young stars who start to believe their own hype and then hit rock bottom when the media decides to write negative stories about them.

Rob doesn't let his family believe the hype that surrounds him, either. Whenever they tell him how proud they are, he always asks them why because he thinks his success is all down to luck.

I is for...

Inspiration

Rob loves watching James Dean and Jack Nicholson movies. Both men really inspired him to become an actor and, in his teenage years, he tried to copy their voices, look and attitude.

He told the *Daily Mirror*: 'Every actor I like is American – I mean, I always say I've stolen things from James Dean's voice, the way he slurs his words, just for chatting up girls and stuff.'

James Dean was the Oscar-nominated actor who plays Jim Stark in the classic *Rebel Without a Cause* (1955). Rob found watching this movie really helped him prepare for *Twilight*. He believes: '*Rebel Without a Cause* was a big influence on the first *Twilight* film – it influenced the hair and stuff. In lots of ways, it has a very similar character arc – an everyday girl brings this relatively strange individual out of his slump.'

James Dean would play the lead in just two other movies: Cal Trask in *East of Eden* (also 1955) and Jett Rink in *Giant* (1956). Tragically, he died in a car crash when he was only twenty-four. Who knows how long his career might have lasted had his life not been prematurely cut short? Dean was the first actor to receive a posthumous Academy Award nomination for Best Actor. All three of his movies were filmed in just over a year.

In May 2009, Rob posed for *GQ* magazine. He wore a leather jacket and, with a cigarette in his hand, he looked the spitting image of James Dean. The stylish photos shot in black and white made his fans drool. He looked *so* hot!

Rob's other favourite actor has enjoyed a much longer career, however: Jack Nicholson has been acting for over fifty years. Rob grew up watching him and says that he has seen every single one of his films. That's a lot of movies because he has appeared in over sixty films. Rob thinks his favourite Nicholson movie has to be *Five Easy Pieces* because he's watched it so many times. Jack Nicholson plays an oil-rig worker called Bobby

ROB'S INSPIRATION IS JAMES DEAN.

Dupea, who gets the news that his father is dying and reluctantly returns home with his pregnant girlfriend. The movie came out in 1970 – that's sixteen years before Rob was even born.

Rob loved Jack Nicholson's character in the movie so much that he borrowed the name Bobby Dupea and used it as his own when performing at open-mic nights in London before *Twilight* made him a big star. He also created a MySpace page under the name Bobby Dupea so that he could post his music up without anyone knowing it came from him.

He told the *Daily Mirror*: 'My favourite actor is Jack Nicholson. I watched *One Flew Over The Cuckoo's Nest* when I was about 13 and I used to try and be him in virtually everything I did. I dressed like him, I tried to do his accent – I think it kind of stuck with me.'

Pretending to be Randle McMurphy from *One Flew Over The Cuckoo's Nest* helped Rob become more confident and outspoken as a teenager. It would be great if he could star in a movie alongside Nicholson one day.

But it wasn't just James Dean and Jack Nicholson who inspired Rob when he was growing up. He also admires the French director Jean-Luc Godard.

'*Prénom Carmen*, which sounds like I'm just saying that to be cool, but it's actually one of my favourite films. I think it's the best Godard film – it's like his version of *Carmen* the opera, one of his films from the eighties. In terms of just pure filmmaking and manipulating an audience, it kind of starts out as a farce, as a complete, stupid farce, with this bank robbery but it's really, really Godardian, with kind of a stupid humour that's so random. Only he could make it, mixed up with these kinds of philosophical elements,' he divulged to Rotten Tomatoes.

Internet

Rob might be one of the most-searched people on the Internet but he really wishes it didn't exist. Although he loves all the fan sites dedicated to him, he thinks the Internet is a massive waste of time. His fans disagree with him, though – they love finding new photos of their hero and chatting to other *Twilight* fans online. The invention of Twitter has allowed fans to communicate with each other really easily and has helped them track Rob down: once a fan spots him out and about, they soon send a tweet to let others know where he is.

Rob told Film.com that he believes: '[The Internet] feeds the worst part of your soul. When you have nothing to do and you go on, when you're too tired to read a book.

'I'll read the news, you go on to the *New York Times*, you get bored and go on IMDb. Then you realise how pathetic you are. I have to delete my history. It is kind of addictive, but at the same time pathetic.'

If ever you find Twitter or Facebook accounts in Rob's name, don't be tricked into thinking it's him. He doesn't have a Twitter or Facebook account. He's only ever posted one tweet and that was using Peter Facinelli's Twitter account. He wrote: 'Hi it's Rob… My first and last tweet. My dad made me do it.' If you want to know what's happening when the *Twilight* movies are being made, it would be a good idea to follow Peter Facinelli – he's constantly tweeting about what the cast are up to.

Interviews

Twilight fans usually start to rate Rob more than Edward Cullen whenever they watch his television interviews and read the funny answers that he gives in magazine interviews. Not only does he have Edward's good looks but he also has a fantastic personality and natural wit.

Some critics are worried that Rob will never be able to escape playing Edward and he'll be forever linked to *Twilight*. He himself doesn't believe this will happen because he's busy making other movies and playing characters that are nothing like Edward Cullen.

Although Rob wants to keep his private life private,

he doesn't mind sharing things with his fans by giving revealing answers in interviews.

'It's such a risky thing, doing interviews. I try to limit the amount of interviews I do. No one is that interesting, especially when you're not really saying anything. And I don't particularly want to be some kind of character in society,' he told *Edge*. 'So, I guess the only thing you can do is do jobs and see if people respond to that. But I'm always holding onto the fact that I don't really know who I am, so hopefully I won't compartmentalise myself because of that. I'm just completely ignorant of the whole thing. I've never really struggled with anything, up until recently. I've got to stop being so self-deprecating 'cos people are starting to believe it. They'll be like, "That guy is an idiot," so I've tried to stop doing that.'

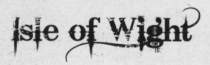

Isle of Wight

The Isle of Wight is a small British island that lies 3–5 miles from England's South Coast in the English Channel. It's also where Rob and Kristen Stewart decided to spend New Year's Eve together and welcome in 2010. At first, this might seem a strange choice of destination because they could have chosen a more exotic location and relaxed together on a beach like so many celebrities do during their winter break. Most

ROB HAD TO DO TONS OF INTERVIEWS TO PROMOTE *TWILIGHT*.

probably, the reason they picked the Isle of Wight is because it's one of the few places in the world that isn't *Twilight*-obsessed and they could walk around unnoticed. They might have thought they wouldn't be spotted, but a young girl saw them outside her local supermarket and bagged herself a snap with Kristen and another with Rob. A few hours later, the photos were on several *Twilight* fan sites and the world's media was on the case.

Despite being spotted, Rob and Kristen didn't let it ruin their fun. Instead, they headed for a party at the Winter Gardens – and it only cost them £3 each to get in. They mingled with the other hundred or so locals and had a really good (and cheap) night. For once, they were just able to be themselves, not movie stars.

Weeks after their trip to the Isle of Wight, it was rumoured they were looking to buy a holiday home there but this seems unlikely as they are so busy filming and promoting their movies that they won't have time to visit the island on a regular basis.

Italy

When Rob was at school he liked looking out of windows and daydreaming. Back then he had no idea how exciting his life would become and that he would have travelled the world before his 25th birthday.

In May 2009, Rob, Kristen, Ashley Greene and a few other members of the *New Moon* cast went to Italy for three intense weeks of filming. This presented a tremendous challenge for director Chris Weitz because everybody knew they would be filming in Montepulciano after Italian fan sites broke the news and so thousands of fans from across the world turned up to watch. Chris needed thousands of extras to don red capes and, having signed up local people, he was eventually forced to ask some foreign *Twilight* fans to stand in when the originals quit. The filming took hours and it was actually quite boring, not to mention unpaid and very hot. Not surprising then that each day some extras failed to return.

Chris revealed on Comic-Con: 'Everywhere where the camera wasn't pointed, there were hundreds of fans there. And it wasn't so much that we minded them being there, it was great. As a matter of fact, people applauded after every take, which is unheard of — it was like doing theatre or something. But it was the sheer logistics of getting through all the fans to get through to where we had to stand by the camera.

'There was one moment where I really had to go to the bathroom, but there was not one single cafe that I could walk into where I wouldn't be mobbed. And by the way, it's not because I'm me, but it's because people were interested if I could set up a meeting with Rob or another member of the cast. So that was quite

difficult, actually, but also intriguing and fun in the same way.'

Rob, Kristen and Ashley still managed to have a great time despite not being able to walk anywhere. They each had two bodyguards and were picked up and driven to the set because so many fans were on the hunt for Rob. Some fans even camped outside their hotel gate. Timing was so tight that Rob only had half an hour for lunch each day and so he couldn't go round signing autographs, either.

Filming the scene where Edward steps into the light and Bella runs through the fountain to save him was very emotional for Rob – it was during this time that he began to understand what the fans feel for Edward and why they found the scene really emotional.

He explained to About.com: 'Just taking that one step into the light, it's been the one moment, since the first Comic-Con, where I've felt the whole weight of anticipation and responsibility to all the people who are so obsessed with the stories. It was a good moment. It was very nerve-wracking, but I probably felt the most in character that I've ever felt, throughout the whole series, at that moment.'

Rob also admitted to feeling a right goofball at having to take his clothes off in front of so many people, like he was doing a striptease, too!

OPPOSITE: ROB IS ALWAYS MOBBED BY FANS.

J is for...

Jackson Rathbone

One really good friend of Rob's is Jackson Rathbone, who plays Jasper in the *Twilight Saga* movies. In fact, he was one of the actors that fans of *Twilight* the book wanted to play Edward. When Stephenie Meyer asked for suggestions on her website, they put forward his name and she included him in her list of possible actors for Edward. Even Jackson admits that he was considered for the part, but he doesn't think he was director Catherine Hardwicke's first choice. Stephenie Meyer's first choice wasn't even Robert Pattinson: she wanted *Stardust* star Henry Cavill to play Edward but, by the time the movie was being made, he was much too old to play a seventeen-year-old schoolboy.

But Jackson isn't at all jealous of Rob and he's happy that he was given the part of Jasper. He told MTV: 'I think he's the best man for the job: I wouldn't have another Edward Cullen than Robert Pattinson, he's perfect.'

Rob and Jackson both love playing their guitars and they've spent many happy hours jamming together. Both are talented musicians with great potential to be successful recording artists. Although Rob doesn't appear with his band Bad Girls any more, Jackson still plays with 100 Monkeys. He's their lead singer and

JACKSON (FAR LEFT) AS JASPER, AND THE REST OF THE CULLEN KIDS.

plays guitar, too. Rob can often be seen at their gigs, supporting Jackson with the rest of the cast.

Jamie Campbell Bower

Jamie Campbell Bower is Caius in the *Twilight Saga* movies. When it was announced that he would play Caius, many *Twilight* fans were thrilled. Jamie has an excellent acting pedigree and they felt that Rob might like having another Londoner in the cast so that he could talk to someone who understood if ever he felt homesick.

When journalists ask Jamie what the real Rob is like, he just says that he's a normal guy, who loves music. He feels for Rob because everyone wants to know everything about him.

Jamie might be British, talented and good-looking but he doesn't believe he'll end up with the Robert Pattinson level of fame. He thinks that people won't fall in love with his character Cauis in the same way as they have Edward Cullen.

Jobs

When he was younger, Rob never knew what job he wanted to do. He has always liked writing scripts, though, and there was a time when he wanted to do political speech writing.

He told the *Los Angeles Times*: 'That's what I wanted to do while I was in school, yeah. I just liked the whole idea of it. I wanted to be involved with politics, that's what my whole plan was. I was going to go to university and then I just thought, "Ah, I can't be bothered to do anything!" [laughs] I don't want to do any more homework!'

In the future, he would like to have one of his scripts produced and maybe release an album, but for now he's just happy to be acting. He likes the fact that acting gives you the freedom to go nuts and it's a lot cooler than working in a shoe shop.

Rob revealed to Gala.de: 'Being a music producer would be the perfect job for me. Or I would like to write. In any case it would be something creative, perhaps also a stockbroker. I like everything hectic.'

Justin Chon

Justin plays Eric Yorkie in the *Twilight Saga* movies and he thinks Rob is a great guy. He was one of the few males in the cast who didn't need to hit the gym to acquire a six-pack. Because he plays one of the humans, not a member of the Cullens or the Wolf pack, he just had to look like a regular high-school guy. Like Rob and Jackson, Justin is also an actor and a musician, but he kept his musical skills a secret at first.

He admitted to *J14*: 'I just didn't even tell anybody. I was just like, "Yeah, I guess everyone plays the guitar so maybe I shouldn't say anything because it doesn't make me special."'

It seems strange that Justin didn't tell Rob: we're sure Rob would have loved having another person to jam with and, anyway, he's such a nice guy. Maybe Justin thought that he wasn't in the same league as Rob and Jackson because they are such talented musicians. Another possible reason was the age gap – Justin is five years older than Rob and Jackson. Whatever, it doesn't stop Justin and Rob hanging out together when the cast go for meals out.

K is for...

Kellan Lutz

Kellan plays Emmett Cullen in the *Twilight Saga* movies and is one of Rob's closest friends on set – the two of them can often be seen messing around. He was one of the main organisers of Rob's 23rd birthday meal in Vancouver. Before the event, he admitted to reporters that he had a big surprise for Rob, but he couldn't tell anyone because that would ruin the surprise. Rob must have been really surprised when he saw his parents at the restaurant.

Kellan gets on so well with his co-star that he wanted to share a room with Rob when he, Kristen and Ashley travelled to Italy to film their Volturi scenes. Shortly before they flew out, he told *Access Hollywood*: 'I'm going and I'm crashing with Rob... I'm going to go do some sight-seeing while he's shooting – I'm going to be that straight-up American tourist.'

Like Rob, Kellan also loves dogs and likes to go jogging with his dog, Kola. Sometimes fans try to jog alongside Kellan but they struggle to keep up with him because he's so fit. Occasionally, he slows down so they don't hurt themselves – quite often, they are female fans in heels! He doesn't mind signing autographs and posing for photos as he likes to spend time with fans and thank them for their support.

Sadly, Kellan and Rob don't get to spend much time together during the *Twilight* promotional tours as Rob is normally sent with Kristen and Taylor in one direction, while Kellan is paired up with Ashley Greene to go somewhere else. Because the *Twilight* movies are massive the whole world over, there are a lot of countries to cover and literally thousands of miles between Rob and Kellan.

Spending a lot of time with Ashley Greene isn't a big problem for Kellan as he's really good friends with the actress. They even worked together in the movie *Warrior* (now in post-production), which was filmed in the window between *Twilight* and *New Moon*. Even when they're not working, Kellan and Ashley like to hang out. They regularly host party nights together and, for

Halloween, they hosted a party at Tao in Las Vegas. Kellan looked so sexy in his skin-tight Batman outfit with built-in muscles and Ashley was gorgeous as a peacock. It was a real shame Rob wasn't there because it would have been nice to see him dressed up as Batman!

Kelly Clarkson

Singer Kelly Clarkson made *Twilight* fans go crazy during a concert when she brought out a cardboard cutout of Rob as Edward Cullen on to the stage. She had just started to sing 'I Want You' when a fan passed it to her. Kelly decided to have fun with the cardboard Rob and started to serenade him, even resting her head on the pretend Rob's shoulder. It was very, very funny.

Kelly thinks the real Rob is cute, even though she hasn't yet had the privilege of meeting him. She told Australian radio presenters Kyle and Jackie O: 'Yes, he's an attractive guy but I think girls are more so into that whole Dracula bit. It's very sexy... I don't know him – I've never really seen him in interviews either... [But] yeah, he's cute.'

Kelly is a big *Twilight* fan and loved reading Stephenie Meyer's books. She was even inspired to write a song for fun with her friends. Her song is called 'Empty As I Am' and it's about Bella and Edward's love. At the moment, there are no plans for it to be released.

Kidnapped

On 10 May 2009, Rob and Kristen were tricked into getting into a phony limo. It was late and they'd been enjoying a night out with some of the other cast members. A fan in a limo had been circling the block, hoping to see them and ask them if they wanted a lift. There were a handful of fans waiting outside the restaurant and, when they heard that Rob and his friends were leaving, they told the limo driver. He joined the taxi queue and, when a waitress came out and helped the cast members into various taxis, Rob and Kristen were ushered into the phony limo.

The fan whisked them away before anyone could tell them that he wasn't an authorised limo driver. Although he delivered them safely to their hotel, lots of fans think this shouldn't have happened. It turned out okay because the man was just a fan and not someone who wished to do the pair any harm. They might have been seriously hurt otherwise.

Kisses

Rob admits that he had his first kiss when he was twelve years old, but he won't reveal who the lucky girl was. However, when he was seventeen, he

ROB GETTING INTO
A CAR IN ITALY.

couldn't find any girls his age to kiss him as they liked bad boys, who were older.

'I had really bad luck with girls [in high school]. The ones I liked hated me and the ones that liked me were not my type. But that's something that I still go through – I like girls that I shouldn't like. But I'm learning and now I take my time before I let the girl know,' he admitted to Spanish *Glamour* magazine.

When Rob decided to become an actor, he had to accept that he would have to kiss lots of girls if the roles required it, even if he didn't fancy them. This might have been a bit of a challenge for him when he was a teenager because he was quite shy back then and struggled to approach girls normally. Thankfully, he's such a good actor that, when he kisses Kristen or any other actress onscreen, it looks so natural. *Twilight* fans always go wild when Edward and Bella kiss as they imagine what it would be like if Rob kissed them.

Rob might have kissed Kristen a lot over the last three years, but, when he filmed *Remember Me* in June 2009, he had to kiss someone else. The lucky girl was *Lost* actress Emilie de Ravin. When they filmed a kissing scene on a New York beach, paparazzi captured the moment and the world's media soon printed the sensational photos. The images of Rob and Emilie lying in the sand in an embrace made some fans wonder how Kristen might feel on seeing her leading man getting

EMILIE AND ROB KISSING ON A NEW YORK BEACH.

close to another woman. Back then, however, Kristen was still thought to be seeing her boyfriend of three years, Michael Angarano.

Millions of fans might dream of being Emilie on that beach, locking lips with Rob again and again, but many will never even get to see Rob in the flesh, let alone kiss him. Two lucky fans did manage to steal a kiss from Rob in May 2009, though – thanks to their generous parents.

Rob was at the Cannes Film Festival at the time and he'd been mingling with some of the biggest stars on the planet. Every great actor and actress was there, promoting their own movie or simply enjoying the great films on offer. Brad Pitt, Jim Carrey and Ben Stiller were all present, treading the red carpet. Poor Rob was at Cannes by himself – none of his *Twilight* cast mates was attending, nor indeed were any of his friends from the *Harry Potter* cast.

One night there was the annual amfAR Cinema Against AIDS 2009 Cocktail Party. As Rob headed there to show his support to such a worthwhile cause, he must have had no idea what was about to happen.

American film producer and movie studio chairman Harvey Weinstein introduced Rob to everyone who was there and admitted that he would love it if the actor would appear in one of his movies one day. Weinstein announced: 'When I first saw *Twilight* with my daughters, I went home the next night and I saw [written] on their doors, Emma Pattinson age eleven, Ruby Pattinson age six and Lily Pattinson age fourteen. All three of my daughters want to marry the guy on my right – I want him to star in a movie for me!'

Rob had to try not to look too embarrassed while Harvey continued: '[He] has agreed to do something extraordinary... I think there is no dad who wouldn't mind Robert Pattinson meeting his daughter, taking a picture with his daughter and just giving her a gentle kiss on the cheek. Somebody in London, New York or LA, there's got to be a dad good enough to bid on that!'

Basic Instinct actress Sharon Stone was hosting the night and also in charge of the auction for Rob's kiss. Before she started the bidding off, Rob jokingly suggested that it should start at $5. As more and more bids came in, everyone began to realise that the kiss was going to raise an amazing amount for charity. In the end, the bidding got so heated that Rob said he would kiss the daughters of *both* bidders if they each gave $20,000. The parents agreed to this and the lucky girls got their kisses!

Kristen Stewart

Although she might have been only seventeen when shooting for *Twilight* started, Kristen Stewart was

BELLA AND EDWARD.

already one of the most experienced members of the cast. She had appeared in fifteen movies, including *Jumper* with Samuel L. Jackson (2008) and *Panic Room* with Jodie Foster in 2002.

Rob told goodprattle.com: 'When I met Kristen, I did the screen test with her and she is very strong. Just naturally, she's not the kind of damsel in distress at all.'

He likes the way that Kristen doesn't back down to people as he shares that character trait. Rob doesn't enjoy backing down one bit, but this can sometimes be hard if he's the only person to feel like that. He knows that if he has a problem during filming then he can turn to Kristen and she will support him.

Because Kristen had been in so many movies, at first Rob felt like he must be professional at all times before he realised that he had a lot more in common with his co-star than he originally thought. He spilled the beans to *Entertainment Weekly*: 'In the beginning I thought to myself, "Because she's so serious, I've got to be really serious." I didn't speak for about two months so I would seem really intense – I would only ever talk about the movie. And I kept recommending all these books. It didn't work, though. Then I started falling apart and my character started breaking down. I felt like an idiot, just following her around, saying, "You really should read some Zola – and there's this amazing Truffaut movie." And she started calling me on things: "Have you actually watched this movie? Yeah? What's it

FANS WOULD LOVE IT IF ROB AND KRISTEN CONFIRMED THEY ARE
TOGETHER IN REAL LIFE.

about?" "It's about a guy on a train." "Did you just look at the photo on the corner of the DVD?"'

When you watch *Twilight* and see Edward and Bella kiss, you can't help but have shivers running down your spine. Their kisses are amazing and look effortless, but Rob insists that's not the case. He spent a lot of time with Kristen talking about the way they should kiss: they both felt that the kissing scenes were the key relationship scenes as well – and that Edward and Bella couldn't kiss like normal people.

He confided in *MTV*: 'The whole thing about both of them is that they think they should be able to, but there's always the elephant in the room. I always want to kill her, like all the time.'

It was quite a challenge for *Twilight* director Catherine Hardwicke to have a leading lady who was just seventeen. Because of her age, Kristen was only legally allowed to work for a maximum of five hours a day. This was really hard for Catherine to deal with because Bella appears in every scene in *Twilight*. Rob and the rest of the cast were so pleased when Kristen turned eighteen that they gave her a birthday cake with 'Now you're on nights' written in icing on the top. That was really funny!

Having Kristen to talk to when *Twilight* was being filmed really helped Rob come out of his shell. Some members of the crew were worried that he'd spent so long getting under Edward's skin that he might be

THE MTV MOVIE
AWARDS MOMENT.

feeling a bit down and miserable so they decided to cheer him up by following him around the set and highlighted passages in the book where Edward smiled or was happy.

Kristen found it quite funny that Rob got so involved in playing Edward that he kind of became Edward all the time, even when the cameras stopped rolling. She told *ET*: 'I had this little thing: "Rob, let's just rehearse the scene all the way through without tearing it down and criticising it." We'd get two lines out, and then he would say, "No, no, no, it's not working!" Rob made himself crazy the whole movie, and I just stopped and patted him on the back through his neuroses. He would punch me in the face if he heard me right now.'

On 31 May 2009 when Rob went to kiss Kristen as they collected their MTV Movie Award for Best Kiss, everyone was shocked when Kristen pulled away, but Rob has since revealed that the fake kiss was all her idea.

If Rob and Kristen aren't actually dating, then they have the kind of close friendship that not many people find in their whole lifetimes. Both of them rate the other's acting ability. Rob says Kristen is the best actress of their generation and she was the reason why he wanted to do *Twilight*. In turn, Kristen says Rob is her perfect Edward – really handsome, sensitive and a great actor.

Kristen declared to *The Advertiser*: 'We went through a lot together. It is crazy to go through something that heavy in real life. At the end of it you are inevitably going to have something. I know a version of him better than anybody else in the world because I did this movie [*Twilight*] with him.'

L is for...

Little Ashes

Rob hasn't only starred in movies made in the UK and USA. In 2008, he travelled to Barcelona in Spain to film *Little Ashes*.

The Spanish-English drama is set in the 1920s and 1930s, and tells the story of three of the most creative talents of that era: Luis Buñuel, Salvador Dalí and Federico García Lorca.

Rob plays Salvador Dalí in the film, which he worked on before being cast in *Twilight*. He is very proud of *Little Ashes* because he took on the challenging role of Dalí, even though he couldn't speak any Spanish.

ROB IN *LITTLE ASHES*.

The movie took a long time to cast and then it was still a couple of years before filming began. Rob had initially been picked to play Federico García Lorca but, a year after he got the part, he was asked to read Salvador Dalí's lines and then, a year after that, the producers told him that they had the funding they needed and filming in Spain would start in four days' time! It's a good job that Rob is a patient person or he might have given up – two years is a long time to wait.

Rob is so glad that he stayed with the project – he loved filming it and thinks the finished movie is great.

He admitted to journalist Laremy Legel: 'I did two little movies last year [*How to Be* and *Little Ashes*]. Without *Twilight*, I don't know what would happen to them. They would get like one theatre, tiny. I love it when people come up to me and say, "I'm not actually a fan of yours from *Twilight*, I'm a fan of yours from the poster of *Little Ashes*." It's so funny.'

Rob wasn't concerned that this wasn't the best-paid movie in the world because he's more interested in a good story than being in the same type of movie all the time.

Obviously, the producers and everyone involved in *Little Ashes* were thrilled when Rob became a massive star because it also meant that more people would get to see their work. They were delighted for Rob, too, because they all enjoyed working with him and thought that he was a great guy.

London

Rob might be living out of a suitcase at the moment, but London will always be his home. He misses being able to walk his dog, as well as all his friends and family who live in the capital.

Rob told *Frida* magazine: 'I landed in London recently, on my way to Rome, and I almost cried because I missed it so much. And I miss my dog. I haven't moved here [to Los Angeles] for good. I live in a rented apartment, where all of the furniture is rented.'

In the future, Rob might have to buy a house in London and another home in Los Angeles – it doesn't look like he'll ever be able to move back to London full time because he's in such demand in America. Maybe his parents will decide to move over to Los Angeles themselves in a couple of years – it must be hard being thousands of miles away from him. If they did join him in Los Angeles, it might help Rob to feel less homesick and it would also be good for him because his mum could help wash his clothes and cook him healthy meals!

Love

One day Rob will fall in love and may consider getting married, but for now he can't imagine being deeply in love. He can't envisage feeling for someone as strongly as Bella and Edward feel for each other.

He explained to goodprattle.com: 'What I always thought was really interesting about Bella is that Edward doesn't really have a choice in how he chooses to love and to live, but Bella's choosing to give

BELLA AND EDWARD
ARE DEEPLY IN LOVE.

up her life, to give up her mortality, which is also something I found very strange about it. I mean, it is essentially how much she wants to be with Edward, but at the same time she has so little regard for [laughs] for remaining human, and they've only known each other for about, what, eight weeks or something? Is that how long the entire story's set? [laughs] I mean, I don't know, and she's already saying, "I don't want to be a human any more" after that! I mean, that's what love is. I always thought Bella's character was really interesting.'

Rob thinks he may end up falling in love with several women because he believes everyone has the right to fall in love again and again. The traditional view of love, where you get married and commit to that person for the rest of your life, seems very unrealistic to our favourite actor and he thinks you can be in love with more than one woman at a time. This might seem a bit of a strange viewpoint, but Rob might feel this way because he's still only young.

Rob is open to finding his perfect woman, though. He told *Bravo*: 'I'm looking for a girl with character. If I find her one day, do you know what I will do? I am going to write her hundreds of love letters.'

Imagine getting a love letter from Rob!

By the way, Rob's auntie Diana thinks he should enjoy being a young man and wait until he's at least forty before he gets married. She told *Life & Style*: 'I don't think it would be a good idea for Robert to be in a serious relationship with Kristen.' Ouch!

Luck

Rob is forever telling his parents that it's just luck that has made him a big star. His fans disagree, however – they think he would have become a massive hit even if he hadn't been cast as Edward Cullen.

Rob is determined to enjoy every minute of fame as he thinks he's so lucky to be experiencing it, as many actors never manage to make a hit movie and he's made several now.

M is for...

Megan Fox

If Rob is the sexiest man on the planet, then Megan Fox has to be the sexiest woman. It was reported the day after the 2009 Academy Awards, on 7 February, that Megan had snubbed Rob at a party when he tried to talk to her. The reports suggest she was more interested in speaking to Andy Serkis, the actor who plays Gollum in the *Lord of the Rings* movies. It's still not known whether the reports were true or if they were made up to try to portray Megan in a bad light.

A few months later, Rob and Megan were at the

MEGAN FOX

Teen Choice Awards in Los Angeles. Together, they collected their surfboards for the Choice Hottie Awards but seemed really happy and there was no awkwardness between them.

Shortly afterwards, it was alleged that Rob and Megan had been on a date together. This really embarrassed Rob. He told *Heat* magazine: 'I read this magazine thing that said, "He was rubbing her back, they were drinking Merlot. He was reading her poetry." I was so embarrassed.'

Some of Rob's friends back in England thought the rumour might be true and texted him about it. He had to admit they hadn't been on a date and that he'd only met Megan once and just briefly.

Megan has also spoken about their alleged relationship. She told *Elle* magazine: 'I just randomly asked someone for a light and it was him. That was the extent of our "relationship".

'He and Zac – they're just too pretty with the big hair and the suits. And Rob is, what, 22? Zac is 21? That's a joke. Boys in their twenties are a waste of time. They have nothing to offer conversationally, they're immature. I feel like I have a better shot with someone in his thirties.'

Ouch, poor Rob! He's one of the wittiest, handsomest guys on the planet – and definitely not a waste of time.

Melissa Rosenberg

Melissa Rosenberg is a talented screenwriter who pens the screenplays for the *Twilight Saga* movies. She was so excited when she met Rob and Kristen for the first time because she knew they would be the ones bringing her words to life.

Melissa told *Hit Fix*: 'When I first saw them, when they were first brought on, I was just stunned at how perfect the casting was. And Catherine [Hardwicke] did a really extraordinary job of finding them. And interestingly when I wrote *Twilight*, before they came on, I [tended to] lean toward humour and sometimes broad humour, sometimes very dark humour so I added a lot of that into the *Twilight* script. It wasn't right. So I actually kind of went a little bit away from the book, I think, in some ways and the actors brought me and the screenplay back into actually more of the tone of the book.'

Melissa has recently told reporters that she thinks people should enjoy what's onscreen and leave Rob's private life to be private.

Merchandise

There might be lots of merchandise with Rob's face on it around, but he doesn't have any say in what gets

BELLA AND EDWARD TURNED INTO DOLLS.

made. No one comes up to him and asks for his approval, which is a bit disappointing for him. He finds it strange that there are Edward Cullen bed covers, toothbrushes and a million other things, so much so that he wants to bring out his own range with hideous photos of himself on it to put people off! He didn't really mind the *Twilight* merchandise too much because he didn't think the images looked all that much like him, but he thinks the *New Moon* images are more like the real him and so he would prefer to have a say in what gets made.

THE TOP FIVE WEIRDEST ROBERT PATTINSON / *TWILIGHT* MERCHANDISE YOU CAN BUY

- Lifesize sticker of Rob's silhouette for your bedroom wall
- Underwear with Rob's face on it
- An Edward Cullen shower curtain
- Forks perfume (smells like 'the air after a thunderstorm has passed')
- *Twilight* plasters (in case of paper cuts!).

Michael Sheen

Michael Sheen plays Aro in the *Twilight Saga* movies. The British actor starred alongside Heath Ledger and

Kate Hudson in *The Four Feathers* in 2002 and with Kate Beckinsale in *Underworld* the following year.

Michael found working with Rob, Kristen and Ashley different from working with other actors and actresses. He told *Empire* magazine: 'It was quite intimidating being on the set with so many young, beautiful people. That was quite extraordinary, being the old, ugly one amongst loads of young, beautiful ones. It's not something I'm used to, really. Not because I'm young and beautiful, but usually there's loads of old, ugly people around me. It was quite encouraging to see how Robert and Kristen are committed to it, how much they put into it and how serious they are about it. They don't take it lightly at all, so that was great to see.'

Michael's daughter Lily is a massive fan of Rob and *Twilight* and her bedroom walls are covered in posters of him and the rest of the cast.

Midnight Sun

When *Twilight* author Stephenie Meyer handed Rob his own copy of *Midnight Sun,* he felt really privileged. The script was top-secret and only a handful of people had seen the version of *Twilight* written from Edward's perspective. Through reading *Midnight Sun*, Rob was able to fully understand how Edward struggles to control his urge to kill.

'In the book [*Twilight*] it seems that when he says, "I'm a monster and I'm going to kill you," and she says, "I'm not afraid," you kind of know the whole time in the book that he's never going to do anything bad. But then you read that first chapter in *Midnight Sun* where the full extent of how much he wanted to kill her and how he's considering killing the entire school just so that he can kill her becomes evident,' he explained to About.com. 'I wanted that element of him to be very prominent. I wanted Bella to be saying, "I'm not scared. You won't do anything to me?" but not so certainly so that it'd suddenly be like, "You won't do anything to me, will you?" I kind of wanted something like that. I think it makes it sexier if there's a very real chance of him just flipping out and killing her.'

Stephenie Meyer was forced to share *Midnight Sun* with the world by releasing it as a download on her official website after it was illegally leaked on the Web. She was really upset because it was just a rough draft and she hadn't finished working on it.

On her official website, she posted: 'So where does this leave *Midnight Sun*? My first feeling was that there was no way to continue. Writing isn't like math; in math, two plus two always equals four, no matter what your mood is like. With writing, the way you feel changes everything. If I tried to write *Midnight Sun* now, in my current frame of mind, James would probably win and all the Cullens would die, which wouldn't dovetail too well with the original story. In any case, I feel too sad about what has happened to continue working on *Midnight Sun*, and so it is on hold indefinitely.'

If you want to check out the partial draft of *Midnight Sun*, you can download it from Stephenie's official website: http://www.stepheniemeyer.com. Any other transcription or reproduction on the Internet is illegal so don't download it from anywhere else.

Miley Cyrus

One of a long list of celebrities who rate Rob is Miley Cyrus. Initially she didn't feel that way and, indeed, told reporters in April 2009 that she wasn't a fan and that girls fall in love with Edward, not Rob. After meeting Rob at the Teen Choice Awards a few months later, she completely changed her mind, however.

She tweeted: 'Gave a hug to Rob Pattinson today. Ok girls, I get it now. So cute. Sorry "Robby" about all my bashing in the past :)'

Modelling

When Rob was twelve, his model-booker mum got him some modelling jobs but he was dropped once his body started to develop. He wasn't all that bothered, though – several of the shoots involved him posing in his pants. Now Rob has become a big movie star, lots of companies will want him to promote their brands. Some people think it's only a matter of time before we see him modelling designer suits and appearing in aftershave ads.

He told *Look* magazine: 'I always looked like a girl up until a few years ago. And I never did any sport, so I was always the kind of gangly guy [laughs].'

If you want to know everything about Rob, you might be interested to know his measurements: he wears size 11 shoes, his waist is 25.5 inches, his chest is 36 inches and he is 6ft 2in tall.

Money

Despite coming from a fairly affluent family, Rob and his sisters were encouraged to get small jobs so they could learn the meaning of money. Rob became a bit of a dog walker for a friend of his mother's and his sister Lizzy had a Saturday job at a nearby library. When Rob

ROB HAS MODEL
GOOD LOOKS –
BUT WE KNEW
THAT ALREADY!

turned ten, he jumped on his bike and started delivering newspapers. At first, he earned around £10 a week, which was a lot of money for a young boy and it soon went to his head. He admits he became obsessed with earning money until he was about fifteen.

While promoting *Harry Potter*, he told reporters that he didn't care for money any more and that he would never do a movie just to make cash. He said he didn't want to make bad movies, but films with great storylines that touch people. Years later, his attitude has stayed the same and he still won't do a movie unless he believes in it.

Rob might not care about money but the press are very interested and they constantly discuss how much money he must be making from the *Twilight* films. This can be frustrating for him, as he explained to *Newsbeat Entertainment*: 'I read some gossip thing saying, because I looked really uncomfortable in a paparazzi photo or something, they're like, "He should get used to it. That's the price to pay if you're getting $12m [£8.1m] a movie." If I'm getting paid $12m a movie I'd walk around naked! That's all nonsense. I don't know who makes that stuff up, even the price for the first one was nonsense.'

Rob won't say how much he has been paid for any of his movies because he likes to keep it private. He has treated himself to one thing, though. He shared with Gala.de: 'I like to take my guitar everywhere. I'm actually quite frugal, but I've bought a 1951 vintage electric guitar after filming *Twilight* in Vancouver. That was the first time in my life that I felt really decadent. Normally, I don't need any luxury. Look at me – I wear the same clothes nearly every day!'

Music

Rob loves songwriting and performing. When fame gets to him, he stays home and writes music. He likes nothing better than chilling at home with his guitar.

Jackson Rathbone (Jasper in *Twilight*) thinks both Rob and Kristen are talented guitarists and he loves to jam with them. They all hang out in Rob's room with Nikki Reed, Kellan Lutz and Ashley Greene.

Rob used to be in a band called Bad Girls, but they never released anything. He told one journalist: 'Bad Girls belonged to my first girlfriend's current boyfriend and he was having an open-mic night. He invited me to sing, but it was just a bit of fun. We only played a couple of gigs. It is just a couple of friends of mine and some other people that I had met fairly recently – we just wanted to start a band for something to do. A lot of my friends are actors and we had so little to do all the time, so, instead of just being bored, we were like, "Why not start a band?" So we did. I had kind of roll-on, roll-off musicians. I still try and play, but it's weird now since

Rob loves music, songwriting and performing.

when I'm trying to do it as an actor, it always seems kind of cheesy.'

Rob has always loved performing at open-mic nights but he had to give them up once fans started to record his performances and put them on YouTube. It just ruined the whole experience for him because the only people he wanted to see him sing and play were in the room, not millions of homes around the world. His open-mic nights were about performing as a musician, not as Robert Pattinson the actor. Now he's stopped performing altogether and will wait a while before he tries again.

In February 2009, Rob did come out of retirement, though – when he bumped into *X Men* star Hugh Jackman in Tokyo. Both were in Japan to promote their respective films and decided to go for a drink together. They ended up doing a late-night karaoke session.

Rob is currently in the process of writing some tracks for a soundtrack, but the name of the movie remains a big secret. He would like to try to have a musical career once his acting career ends.

He shared with radio host Elvis Duran: 'I was just doing music for fun – I never wanted a career out of it. I mean, my sister's a singer and I've seen what the music industry's like, and it's impossible.'

Rob does have a few musical secrets, though. He told *Look* magazine: 'I played in some pizza restaurants in London for a few years and it was the coolest thing I'd ever done. I still find it very therapeutic. It's one of the most relaxing things you could possibly do.'

He has always been very musical and first started to play the piano at three years old. When he was five, he took up the guitar as well but stopped at the age of twelve.

After appearing in *Harry Potter*, Rob decided to start playing again and to try to write some music of his own with friends. He describes his musical style as being a bit like his two favourite artists, Van Morrison and Jeff Buckley. Rob loves music, but he doesn't know much about contemporary artists and music. His iPod is not filled with Lady Gaga and Rihanna tracks, but classic songs from blues legends John Lee Hooker and Elmore James.

In *Twilight*, Rob plays the piano and he plays guitar in *How to Be*. Actually, it was quite challenging for him to play the guitar in *How to Be* because he had to pretend to be no good at it!

How did two of Rob's songs end up on the *Twilight* soundtrack?

Rob is a very private person and, to start with, he wasn't at all comfortable with *Twilight* director Catherine Hardwicke even listening to his music. She had heard rumours that his songs were really good but, when she asked him about it, he always brushed her off.

During a guest DJ spot with KCRW Radio,

Catherine admitted: 'I kept asking him every day, can I hear your music? Maybe we can somehow use it in the movie. And he was very reluctant – "No, you know, let me try and record something." He'd say, "Oh, I'll bring something tomorrow that I think might be good for the movie." Tomorrow he didn't bring it; the next day, he never brought it to me.

'He was very shy about letting me hear it and, finally, a friend of mine, Carl Liker, who lives in Venice, who has the funkiest little studio inside his apartment and I said, "Come on over here – I mean, Carl wears flip flops and shorts, man. You know it's not intimidating, just sit down on the tiny little Japanese chair he has and just play a few songs and let's hear it."'

Catherine was really impressed and decided 'Let Me Sign' would be perfect for the scene where Edward sucks the venom from Bella's arm and 'Never Think' would suit the restaurant scene when Edward tells Bella that he can read minds. Catherine has since admitted that watching Rob play his own music was one of her favourite parts of making *Twilight*. She says: 'He just lets it out and it breaks your heart.'

Even now, Rob is a bit shocked at the response to his tracks. It took him and two of his friends just three minutes to write 'Let Me Sign'. Fans have been urging him to release a solo album, but Rob says it's not going to happen – just yet.

He explained to *Virgin Media*: 'I don't think people

should look for a contract. My sister works so hard to make money and I think it ruins you. I think it's a lot easier to make money in the acting world, not that it's easier but there aren't so many pressures on you. You don't have to be so humble, where in the music industry you have to really bow down to a lot of people to get noticed.'

And if he does decide to release a solo album, then he plans to use a pseudonym so that people will buy it because they like his music, not because he is Robert Pattinson.

'I might make an album, but not through a record company or anything. I'd like to do something independent. I'd just like to have it just for myself so I can work with good musicians and stuff,' he declared to MovieOnline.

N is for...

Nakedness

Rob has admitted that he would get naked for the right role. In doing so, he would be joining the likes of Ryan Reynolds (*The Proposal*), Ralph Fiennes (*Red Dragon*) and John Cleese (*A Fish Called Wanda*).

However, Rob thinks that not many people would really like to see him naked because it would shatter their illusions. Millions of *Twilight* fans might disagree, however. They would love to see him naked in *Breaking Dawn*.

Although Rob is prepared to strip off, he would find it a tough call because he's actually rather shy about his body. Indeed, he found filming some of the scenes for *Little Ashes* quite embarrassing.

In an interview with *Star* magazine, he said: 'It's funny because Spanish people have no problem with nudity at all, and I mean at all. And English people obviously do have the most enormous problem with it. Little things, like when I saw my father getting changed for swimming, I was traumatised by it… I kind of freaked out a bit.'

New Moon

For Rob, Kristen and the rest of the cast, *New Moon* meant a new director. Catherine Hardwicke impressed everyone with her directing skills on *Twilight* and was subsequently asked if she would direct *New Moon*, but she refused. Despite being offered a lot more money, she believed the fast turnaround wouldn't give her enough time to prepare and she didn't want to do something that would let down Stephenie Meyer or the *Twilight* fans themselves.

The Golden Compass director Chris Weitz was brought in to replace Catherine in December 2008 and set about putting his own mark on Edward and Bella's story. Filming moved from Portland in the USA to Vancouver, Canada, because the production team didn't feel that Portland could cope with *New Moon* and

Eclipse being filmed back-to-back and the lower Canadian dollar also made Vancouver a cheaper option.

Rob couldn't wait to shoot the movie because *New Moon* is his favourite book in the *Twilight Saga*, even though his own character hardly appears in it. He told fans at Comic-Con: 'I think that *New Moon* was my favourite book as well [agreeing with Kristen] mainly

BELLA AND EDWARD IN A FLASH FORWARD SCENE FROM *NEW MOON*.

because I like the juxtaposition... It's such a hyped character, Edward, and there are so many people looking at him like a romantic hero. In *New Moon*, the way that I read it anyway, he's just so humbled. It's a character who's looking at Bella and thinking that he loves something too much, but he can't be around. He deliberately starts breaking up their relationship, which I think is a very relatable thing and is very kind of painful.'

The fight sequence with the Volturi right at the end of the movie was Rob's favourite scene for two reasons: he liked doing the scene physically and also because Bella is the one who saves Edward, not the other way around. Edward is supposed to be the hero of the story, but it's Bella who saves him.

Chris Weitz was presented with quite a challenge in *New Moon* — he had to try to give Rob more screen time without damaging the integrity of the story. Rob was the major reason why *Twilight* was such a success and so he needed a bigger role in *New Moon* to satisfy the fans.

In the book, Bella hears Edward's voice but, in the movie, Chris decided to have Edward appear in hallucinations so more of Rob could be seen. This also prevents the story from being too cheesy.

Filming *New Moon* was tough for Rob and Kristen because they were under so much pressure. During the making of *Twilight*, no one knew how big it would become and so the whole cast thought it would just be a small movie. With *New Moon*, they knew people would be expecting even more and they couldn't afford to mess up.

Nicknames

Rob and Robert are the two main names that our favourite actor goes by, but he has also been given the nicknames RPattz and Spunk Ransom.

Millions of girls might love the name Robert, but Rob himself hates it and wishes he had a different name! In fact, he dislikes his name so much that he wants no reference to it. His fans have nicknamed him RPattz because it's easier and quicker to type on forums than Robert Pattinson. Rob isn't a big fan of that name either, but thinks it's okay because 'at least it's not an insult – it sounds kind of like antacid or something,' he told MTV. 'I'd like to be called "Ransom Spunk" or "Spunk Ransom."'

Rob has taken other names when checking into hotels and he used the name Bobby Dupea when he performed a one-off acoustic set at the Whisky-A-Go-Go club in Los Angeles. Bobby Dupea was the name of the character played by Jack Nicholson in the film *Five Easy Pieces* – a movie Rob loves. Before he became famous, Rob had a MySpace page where he pretended to be a musician by that name and he used to post up his own songs for people to listen to.

#

Nikki plays Rosalie in the *Twilight Saga* movies. Like Rob, she too struggled at first to accept that she was playing one of the most beautiful vampires in the world – it was a lot to live up to. She admits that she sometimes feels as if she needs to apologise to young fans when they ask her questions. Rob might have hated having to spend two hours each day whitening himself up, but Nikki had an even harder time – she is naturally brunette with dark features. To play Rosalie, she had to completely transform herself.

During the filming of *New Moon*, the media suggested Nikki was really jealous of Kristen Stewart because she wanted Rob to herself but this was all lies. Nikki managed to set the record straight during an interview with *Seventeen* in October 2009. She told them: 'I can't win. A few weeks ago I was at this event, and they said, "You missed Rob's birthday, how do you feel?" And I said, "I called him, it's fine." And they wrote, "She's clearly bitter over the breakup." I'm like, what breakup? Rob and I were never together. My opinion of Rob has always sort of been the same. He's a great guy, he's really talented, [but] we're not as close as the rest of the cast.'

It's nice that Nikki has told everyone the truth and fans now know she and Rob were never an item.

NIKKI AS ROSALIE.

O is for...

Oregon

Rob didn't want to let his director Catherine Hardwicke down and so, as soon as he got the part of Edward Cullen, he started preparing and learned everything he could about *Twilight* and his character. Some people say he had become too obsessed when he moved to Portland, Oregon, two months before anyone else arrived on set.

Oregon was thought to be the perfect place to film *Twilight* because it's often-cloudy skies fitted with the town, Forks, where the story is set. Everything didn't go to plan, though, because filming was often interrupted by the bad weather, which could change from sunny to stormy in an instant.

Rob told Hollywood.com: 'Oregon has the strangest weather stuff that happens, especially in the spring when we were shooting. It would be, like, sunny, snowing, raining and hailing at exactly the same time. Though it could be raining, there'd be no clouds in the sky and stuff. I don't know, it was like fake weather.'

He wasn't the only one to find filming in Oregon challenging, either. Even the highly experienced

THE SCENERY IN THE *TWILIGHT* MOVIES IS BEAUTIFUL THANKS TO THE STUNNING LOCATIONS.

Catherine Hardwicke found it tough. She struggled so much that she was in tears on some of the days. She soon stopped crying once she saw the dedicated fans who stood watching in the pouring rain and hail: she knew she must pull herself together for their sakes and also for Stephenie Meyer to ensure the movie was the best she could make it.

Oscars Night

When Rob was asked to present at the 2009 Oscars, he thought it must be a joke. He hadn't expected to get an invite, let alone be asked to present alongside the lovely star of *Mamma Mia!* Amanda Seyfried. As he made his way into the venue, Rob felt really nervous on the red carpet – he'd messed up the rehearsal and thought he was going to be the biggest letdown. Actually, he did a great job and, hopefully, he'll be asked to present again in the near future. On camera, he seemed relaxed, despite the fact that over 36 million had tuned in to the Awards.

He told Fandango: 'I got there and then I'm sitting in the second row. It was unbelievable – I keep thinking that something terrible is going to happen. "Death" is the only thing I'm thinking the whole time. I just used up all my luck, so I'm probably going to die at 23 or something.'

ROB AND AMANDA SEYFRIED PRESENTING AT THE OSCARS.

In fact, viewing figures for the Oscars went up by 4 million from the previous year and the increase was said to be down to Rob and Zac Efron attracting a younger audience. After the show, Rob was seen chatting to Zac, Vanessa Hudgens and quite a few of the other big names. It was just a shame that Kristen Stewart wasn't there to keep him company. It must have been really strange for Rob to meet some of the biggest movie stars on the planet without Kristen or one of his other friends by his side.

P is for...

Peter Facinelli

In the *Twilight Saga* movies, Peter Facinelli plays Dr Carlisle Cullen. He is one of the oldest cast members, being more than ten years older than Rob, Kristen, Ashley and most of the other actors and actresses on set. As well as being that bit older, he has a lot more responsibility: he's also a husband and father to three young girls.

Rob gets on really well with his *Twilight* dad (Peter describes him as a good, solid guy) and often they will catch up and grab a bite to eat together after long days on set. Peter loves to make the media look foolish and,

PETER FACINELLI [CENTRE] AS DR CARLISLE CULLEN.

when the photos of Rob and Kristen allegedly holding hands at a Paris airport were published, he tweeted: 'Co-stars caught holding hands. Guess this picture proves everything.' The photo he posted wasn't of Rob and Kristen holding hands though, but of himself and Kellan Lutz holding hands. It was very funny!

Plays

Rob has been in quite a few plays during his relatively short acting life. He also appeared in the odd production or two at school, even though acting didn't interest him then – most children have to perform in the school play at some point. When he first joined the Barnes Theatre Club when he was fifteen he didn't start off acting, but worked backstage for quite a while before landing a small part in their production of *Guys and Dolls*.

Rob told *Scholastic*: 'Rusty and Ann, who are the directors, were actors themselves and were very talented. They were a very good group, and for some reason, when I finished the backstage thing, I just decided that I should try to act. So I auditioned for *Guys and Dolls* and got a little tiny part as some Cuban dancer or something, and then in the next play I got the lead part, and then I got my agent. So I owe everything to that little club.'

Rob never forgets the people who helped him get where he is today. Often he tells reporters that he owes everything to the Barnes Theatre Club and that some of his best acting was in their productions.

Once Rob got an agent, he didn't stop doing plays altogether. While the agent searched for television roles, Rob auditioned and won a part in a professional production of William Shakespeare's *Macbeth*. He didn't have to travel too far to perform – its venue was the Old Sorting Office on the common near his house! This was his first experience of performing to a large crowd.

For a while, Rob didn't do plays as he was much too busy filming *Vanity Fair* and *Harry Potter*, but, once things calmed down again, he decided that he needed to do more theatre in order to learn how to really act. At this point, he secured a part in the black comedy *The Woman Before*, alongside established actress Helen Baxendale [Emily in *Friends*]. Things didn't go to plan, though.

Rob shared with EW.com: 'At the time I really thought, "Wow, I must be great, I'm like f******* Brando!" I had this special idea where "I'm going to be a weirdo, this is how I'm going to promote myself." And then, of course, I ended up getting fired.'

Rob has never revealed why he was fired shortly before the first performance on 12 May 2005 and it remains a mystery.

Premières

Poor Rob had such a bad time at his first première that it's surprising he didn't pack acting in altogether. He was so excited after filming *Vanity Fair* in 2004 that he

ROB AT THE *HARRY POTTER* PREMIÈRE.

couldn't wait to see the movie on the big screen, but his scenes were cut out and he only appears on the DVD version.

'It was my first real job. I went along to the première, but nobody had told me that I had been cut out. I didn't realise until the film ended,' he told the *Irish Times*. 'The casting agent was the same one who did *Harry Potter*. They felt so bad about it – they gave me an early meeting for the next *Harry Potter* film. And that went well.'

Although Rob was really humiliated at the première, looking back he must be glad now as he landed the part of Cedric Diggory off the back of it.

Rob's *Harry Potter* première was another real eye-opener for the actor because a few hours earlier he had been able to walk around unnoticed in Leicester Square, but at the première he had thousands of fans calling his name. He was one of the only stars not to wear designer clothes – instead he opted for a vintage red velvet jacket and leather trousers.

Rob really struggled to cope at the Los Angeles *Twilight* première. Thousands upon thousands of fans were screaming his name and, everywhere he looked, photographers and reporters tried to get his attention. Indeed, he was so shaken up that, ten minutes into the screening, he was forced to leave and had a panic attack in his car.

Rob might have been to dozens of *Twilight* premières

across the world now, but he's still shocked at the response that he receives and thinks he will never get used to girls screaming at him. He told the *Los Angeles Times*: 'When you're greeted by crowds of screaming fans, it's like being in some medieval battle. I guess that's the closest analogy, especially after yesterday. A ton of people ran down the street outside the Apple Store. I felt like I was literally being charged by Celts.'

Sadly for Rob and the rest of the cast, there was only one première for *New Moon* and that was in Los Angeles. All the cast members loved going to the different *Twilight* premières and so it was a shame there was only one for *New Moon*. Even though other countries didn't have premières of their own, the fans still turned up to see Rob and co. at events. In Munich, 20,000 people arrived, just to get a glimpse of them. Wow!

Preparation

Before *Twilight* made Rob the massive star that he is today, he liked to head down to his local coffee shop with new scripts and work on them there. He enjoyed being around people and the noise helped him, too. These days he has to prepare in his hotel room or trailer instead.

At the moment, Rob's so busy that he only has a few weeks between movies and so he must quickly prepare for roles. At this point in his career, he can't afford to take whole months off to research and understand a character before shooting begins.

Publicist

Rob is a bit obsessive about his work and refuses to take advice from anyone. It's because of this that he will never hire a publicist.

He explained to America's *People* magazine: 'I have very, very specific ideas about how I want to do my work and how I want to be perceived, to the point of ridiculousness sometimes.

'I don't listen to anyone else. That's why I don't have a publicist – I can't stand it if someone's trying to tell me to do something which might be a mistake.'

Q is for...

Q & A

In the last year and a half, Rob has done literally thousands of interviews. His fans want to find out everything there is to know about him. Sometimes interviewers focus on the movie that he happens to be promoting, sometimes they ask him about his personal life and sometimes they just try to have fun.

Here are some interesting questions and answers from Rob's Q & As:

Q: Who is your celebrity crush?

A: Kristen Stewart.

Q: How much is in your wallet?

Are they or aren't they?
Rob and Kristen together for
the première of *Twilight*.

Taylor, Kristen and Rob win big at the 2009 MTV Movie Awards.
Rob won Breakthrough Performance (Male).

Above: Rob strikes a pose at the Cannes Film Festival 2009 to promote *New Moon*.

Below: Whispering something in Kristen's ear at a concert in Germany.

Filming on the set of *Remember Me* (2010) in New York. Rob is a natural in front of the cameras. Fans were worried when it looked like Rob had gotten injured on set [see *inset*] but it turned out to be just for the movie.

Despite having a fear of crowds, Rob is a pro on the red carpet and never disappoints his adoring fans.

During the promotion of *The Twilight Saga* movies, Rob's face was on the cover of practically every magazine.

Here he is on the December 2009 issue of *Vanity Fair*.

Left: On the cover of a *Life Story – The Real Boys of Twilight* special edition, alongside Kellan Lutz and Taylor Lautner.

Right: *Entertainment Weekly* published three editions of their December 4, 2009 issue, called 'Team Edward', 'Team Jacob' and 'Team Bella'.

Just try taking your eyes off him! Rob is the most gorgeous celebrity in Hollywood today… any Rob fan will surely agree.

A: Thousands of dollars.

Q: What don't you understand about girls?

A: Why they love Ugg boots!

Q: What's your favourite girly movie?

A: *Pippi Longstocking.*

Q: Worst habit?

A: Speaking too much.

Q: What was your last dream about?

A: Kristen Stewart.

Q: Wizard or vampire?

A: Wizard.

Q: Favourite food?

A: I like all fast food, but my favourite is probably In-N-Out Burger.

Q: If you could swap places with someone, who would it be?

A: Someone who has lots of respect or power – George Bush, possibly.

Q: If you couldn't have played Edward, which other character would you have picked?

A: James, that's the only other character I would have liked to have played.

Q: Which superpower would you pick?

A: The ability to stop and start time. I don't really want many superpowers because, once you have superpowers, people will just say, 'Hey, can you use your superpowers for this?' It's like having money: once you have loads of money, everyone's like, 'Can I borrow some money?' It's like, I don't want to give you any of my superpowers, all right.

Q: If you could have any vampire trait, what would it be?

A: Jumping! I was thinking I'd like to have a suit for jumping – that'd be quite cool, if I could jump really high. I'd be jumping around all the time. I'd probably get bored of it after a while.

R is for...

Remember Me

As soon as filming on *New Moon* wrapped, Rob headed to New York to shoot the movie *Remember Me*. He plays the lead (Tyler) who falls in love with Ally (played by *Lost* actress Emilie de Ravin) when both suffer the loss of one of their family. Pierce Brosnan is Rob's onscreen dad and he was given a little sister to look after, too. Fans flocked to New York to try to see Rob but they were kept at arm's length by security because time was tight: he had to make sure he'd finished filming by August 2009 so that he could jet back to Vancouver to start work on *Eclipse*.

Rob got on really well with Emilie and both actors caused a stir when they filmed making-out scenes on a beach and hung out at a fairground, too. In the film, Tyler (Rob) wins Emilie's character (Ally) a massive panda cuddly toy.

Ring of the Nibelungs

Rob's second movie was *Ring of the Nibelungs* and involved him living in South Africa for three and a half months. At the time, he was only seventeen and so he must have found it strange to be away from his family for so long.

He plays the part of Giselher, younger brother of Princess Kriemhild (Alicia Witt) and King Gunther (Samuel West), in the tale of a young blacksmith who slays a dragon, wins the heart of a warrior queen, but then receives some cursed treasure which threatens to ruin his new life with the woman he loves. The story has strong links with J.R.R. Tolkien's *Lord of the Rings* – both are based on the same German myths.

The television movie was produced for a German audience but released in the UK, USA and Australia under different titles. These included *Dark Kingdom: The Dragon King*, *Curse of the Ring*, *Sword of Xanten* and *Die Nibelungen*. It came out in Germany in

November 2004 but British audiences didn't get to see it until December 2005.

Rob didn't use his earnings from the *Ring of the Nibelungs* and *Vanity Fair* to buy himself a car or to go on a fancy holiday. Instead, he sensibly used the money to pay for his college fees.

Romance

Being romantic doesn't come naturally to Rob, but he tries his best. He knows that girls love romantic gestures and so he has shown his romantic side in the past, although things didn't go to plan.

Indeed, our favourite heartthrob once admitted to reporters: 'I can't think of a single romantic thing that I've ever done. I would never serenade someone to be romantic – you have to have so much balls to do that!

'I put a flower in someone's locker when I was fifteen years old, this girl called Maria. She thought that it was someone else and the other guy claimed it as well, which is great!'

Rob might not like taking girls to the cinema on dates but he will still watch romantic films every now and again.

He disagrees with people who think the *Twilight Saga* movies need more action in them if they are to appeal to guys. Rob doesn't believe this is the case as

Edward is very romantic with Bella.

some boys like a bit of romance and don't just want fights and violence in a film. In fact, some guys enjoy *Twilight* so much that they have visited Forks where the series is set and the most devoted have set up their own *Twilight* websites. Head over to Twilightguy.com if you want a guy's take on all things *Twilight*. It's really interesting and Kaleb Nation's red carpet videos are awesome.

Rob added: 'I've watched *Titanic* and I didn't think, "Oh, this is a girls' film." Especially in *New Moon*, and actually in the whole series, I've never played it thinking, "Oh, I'm in a series of girls' films and I'm doing something just for girls." I don't feel like I'm doing an animated *Tiger Beat* every week: I like doing romantic scenes, I felt like a lot of the storyline in *New Moon* is very heartbreaking and true. I didn't think I was doing something just for the sake of romance – I thought, in a lot of ways, that it was a really sad story.'

It's so great that Rob has a sensitive side and doesn't pretend to be macho, like some actors do. It would be nice if he combined romance and action one day and played James Bond. He'd be a great replacement for Daniel Craig later on. Ashley Greene and Nikki Reed would make great Bond girls too – but maybe Kristen wouldn't agree!

Rumours

Chances are you will have read several stories about Rob in the press and believed what the magazine or website said was true and really did happen. Sadly, because Rob is such a big star now and stories about him and his life encourage millions of fans to buy copies of publications every week, some magazines choose to print stories that don't contain a shred of truth in them. Every now and again, sick websites and blogs report that Rob has died just to scare *Twilight* fans. They don't seem to care that they are causing Rob and those who love him pain.

One of the biggest rumours was started in June 2009 when news broke that Rob had narrowly avoided being hit by a taxi in New York after fans chased him on to a busy street. Reporters loved the story and, in a matter of minutes, it spread right across the world. Poor Ashley Greene was asked how Rob was doing on the red carpet at an event just a few hours later. She hadn't heard anything about the accident and so it must have been quite bewildering for her to learn what happened from a reporter – and she would have been very concerned about Rob, too. It's a wonder she didn't stop what she was doing and try to ring her friend straight away.

Rob told *Access Hollywood* about the New York traffic

ROB SOMETIMES GETS OVERWHELMED BY FAN ATTENTION.

accident: 'It was the most innocuous situation. I think the cab may have been stationary – I may have just walked into the cab. It was entirely blown out of proportion: they were saying there were mobs of screaming fans, there were no fans there, it was like four o'clock in the morning… and it was just one paparazzi who couldn't get a photo.'

Another horrible rumour that really upset Rob's mum was when it was reported that her son had experienced a heroin overdose.

To another journalist, Rob added: 'I also had a "heroin overdose" in New York as well, which was an exciting one for my mum. I had been working so hard, my mum calls me up so much, but I didn't answer the phone and when I found out afterwards when one of the security guys from the film came, he ran into my room and I was like, "What are you doing? You could have knocked!" It was on a very legitimate news source, so bizarre.

'The thing is, people read it. I'm so ignorant I just think, "No one reads this stuff anyway, I'm the only one who reads it." Sometimes you get quite frustrated by it… everything goes away.'

Rob does well to keep calm when magazines print such lies. Some stars have taken magazines and newspapers to court for printing allegations about them and they've received substantial compensation, too. Rob hasn't done so yet but this might be something that he has to consider in the future. At the moment he just shrugs off the rumours and lies, but in a few years' time when he perhaps has a family of his own, he might decide to take publications to court if they print lies about his family.

Rob has such a great sense of humour that, when he was asked at a press conference what was the weirdest or funniest thing he'd ever read or heard about himself, he replied: 'Recently, some magazine had on the cover that I was pregnant. I was just like, "Wow!" And it was without a hint of irony or anything. I didn't really know what to make of that one. I don't even know if that qualifies as libellous because they can just say, "Well, it's obviously fiction," but it's written in a non-fiction magazine. I saw a couple of comments under the article saying, "That's why he always wears jackets. He always wears layers to hide it."'

Running

Rob hates sports and he's terrible at all of them apart from maybe jogging. He used to like going jogging to unwind, but he can't do this much any more because fans would follow him.

At a recent press conference, Kellan Lutz enjoyed telling *Twilight* fans that Rob came last when the whole *Twilight* cast went for a run shortly before a scene.

ROB RUNNING ON THE SET
OF REMEMBER ME.

RUPERT GRINT

Ashley Greene has also poked fun at the real Edward Cullen, telling fans that Rob runs like a mountain goat.

Rob is so laid back that he doesn't mind what his fellow cast members say about him. 'Mountain goat? [laughs] I would have said that I run more like a cheese string! What does a mountain goat run like?' he asked MTV. 'That is much more athletic than the way I run. I run like a person who has just had their limbs sewn together – I'm not even like a human!'

Even Kristen Stewart thinks she is more athletic than Rob and claims he can hardly skip, let alone do anything else. She even nicknamed him Flippy because she thinks he looks like a penguin flapping its wings when he tries to do stunts.

Rob doesn't even try to argue with his co-star and told *Harper's Bazaar*: 'You notice it in the film [*New Moon*], she looks so much more athletic than I do. And I'm supposed to be the superhero.'

Poor Rob! We think he looks fit, despite what Kristen, Kellan and Ashley say.

Rupert Grint

Rob and Rupert Grint (Ron Weasley from *Harry Potter*) may go back a long way but they are rumoured to be competing to play Prince Harry in a biopic of his life, *The Spare*. Keira Knightley's boyfriend Rupert

Friend is also said to be in the running, but it looks as if Rob will be the one given the nod by director Peter Kosminsky.

Even if Rob doesn't get the part, we're sure that he won't hold anything against his *Harry Potter* chum if he gets it instead: Rupert really helped him settle in during his first week on the *Harry Potter* set.

It's thought they keep in touch with each other via text messages and Rob made Rupert promise to read *Twilight* after he won a bet. Rupert didn't realise there were four books in the series! Like Rob, Rupert isn't just interested in making big blockbusters but is also keen to work on smaller movies with really good storylines. Aside from *Harry Potter*, Rupert has played Ben Marshall in the coming-of-age movie *Driving Lessons* in 2006 and wild-boy Malachy in *Cherrybomb* (2009). It would be great if Rob and Rupert could work on something together again sometime soon.

S is for...

Schedule

Since *Twilight* first came out, Rob's schedule has been so packed that he hasn't had time to change anything. Just a month after the promotional tour ended, he was presenting at the 2009 Oscars – *Twilight* really did turn his life upside down.

Since then, he has been followed everywhere by gangs of screaming girls but he has become better at hiding behind people so they can't spot him in public places when he's enjoying free time away from his busy schedule.

His *New Moon* shooting schedule was a lot less

hectic than those of Kristen Stewart and Taylor Lautner because he was in fewer scenes in the second *Twilight* movie. This meant that he found filming a lot less intense.

Rob explained to the press: 'There's been a bunch of things that have made it easier. One thing, it's my favourite book. I understood everything about it – well, not everything but a lot of it. I had a really specific way of how I wanted to play it, which influenced the way I played the first one and the third one. The second book I really connected to really quickly, and also I had months and months from *Twilight* to ruminate on that and I'd seen it... It was nice because I knew what I wanted to fix. You do that with every job you do, you notice things that need to be fixed. I improve on that, I think it's an improvement. It was nice actually not being the lead because I could implement the changes... I think it was an older performance.'

Filming of *Breaking Dawn* needs to fit in with Rob's very busy schedule and will probably take place in the autumn of 2010 at the earliest. Because the book is so long, the story might be split into two – so the second *Breaking Dawn* movie will probably be filmed in the spring of 2011. It will be hard for *Twilight* fans to wait that long.

But Rob doesn't seem to have any issues with his busy *Twilight Saga* schedule. He divulged to journalist

Rebecca Murray: 'There's nothing really scary about the franchise itself: I like all the people I work with, I generally have very few disagreements about the script or anything while we're doing it, especially on *New Moon*. It just seemed so relaxed and easy. I've been on three different sets since 14 January. I've had, like, three days off. I'm going to be on set all next year as well. I don't know what doing errands and things is really like 'cos I haven't had a sustained period of time where I've been off – I don't know how it's really changed. I still feel like I'm pretty much exactly the same, which is maybe not a good thing.'

School

Rob's first school was Tower House Preparatory. It's an independent boys-only establishment for pupils aged four to thirteen in East Sheen, southwest London. He might be the best actor on the planet right now but he certainly wasn't the best-behaved pupil during his time there.

He revealed all in an interview with the *Sunday Times*: 'I wasn't with the cool gang, or the uncool ones. I was transitional, in between. I was never a leader, and the idea of my ever being made head boy would have been a complete joke. I wasn't involved in much at school and I was never picked for any of the teams. I wasn't at all focused at school and I didn't achieve much, but I've got a sense of urgency now. I feel I can't let any more time waste away.'

Rob moved to the £4,000-a-term Harrodian School in Barnes when he was twelve. It was the first time that he had girls in his school and he describes this as a big turning point in his life. He told *Newsround*: 'I became cool and discovered hair gel.'

In one school newsletter he was described as the 'runaway winner of last term's Form Three untidy desk award'. Not much has changed since then – he's still messy!

When Rob was fourteen he decided to form a rap group with two of his friends. He shared with the *New York Times*: '[It was] pretty hardcore for three private school kids from suburban London.' They used to practise at Rob's house but they didn't get much privacy. 'And my mum's, like, cramping our style, popping her head in to ask, "You boys want a sandwich?"'

When he wasn't at school or hanging out with his friends, Rob liked to watch *Doctor Who* or play computer games. He also enjoyed watching *Sharky and George* and *Hammertime* cartoons.

His favourite teacher at school was his English teacher because she got him interested in writing and didn't mind marking his long, rambling answers that went on for pages and pages. Despite the fact that he liked his teachers and turned up for lessons, Rob's school reports were never very good and always said he didn't try too hard. He has since admitted that he was even expelled from school when he was twelve.

Rob confessed to the *Daily Mirror*: 'I was at a small private school in London: I wasn't very academic. My dad said to me, "Okay, you might as well leave since you're not working very hard." When I told him I wanted to stay on for my A-levels, he said I'd have to pay my own fees, then he'd pay me back if I got good grades.'

ROB IN HIS SCHOOL PICTURE.

Rob used his pay cheques from *Vanity Fair* and the *Ring of the Nibelungs* to pay for his education and he ended up doing really well in his exams, coming out with an A and two Bs – but his dad still didn't pay him back. Rob is proof that you shouldn't listen to people who pull you down.

Even though Rob got really high grades, he doesn't know how he managed this! He had been busy filming abroad, hadn't had much time to revise and only knew about half the syllabus.

Rob might not like to admit that he's clever, but he really is. He reads books that are too heavy for the majority of people, watches films that not many people have heard of and some of the words that he uses in his answers in interviews are very intellectual.

Scriptwriting

In the future Rob would like to have his own production company and write movie scripts. It's thought that one script based on diaries he kept when he was younger might be made into a movie in the near future.

Rob has already penned several scripts so he knows what he's talking about. He might be one of the most successful actors in the world, but he still wants more. He sets himself targets and goals for the things that he wants to achieve in his life and admits that he wants to have his own production company by the time he is twenty-six.

If Rob does set up on his own, he won't be the first big name to do so: Brad Pitt has his own production company (Plan B), Smokehouse is run by George Clooney and *Twilight* star Taylor Lautner has his own production company with his dad. It's not known what name Rob will give his production company, but Bobby Dupea must surely be a strong contender because he has used that name in the past and loves Bobby Dupea in the Jack Nicholson movie *Five Easy Pieces*.

And, if you're wondering why Rob wants to own his own production company, then it's because he wants to change the way the film industry works. He told philly.com: 'I guess I'm just a control freak. I don't like the way the film industry is. If you come with a good script and then it goes to the studios and gets financing, it all gets changed because they want to make money. And it's, like, how do you know if it's going to make money or not? All you're doing is making it generic when you do that, and making it generic is no guarantee that it's going to make money, either. The only way to abandon that is to take risks.

'And you need to be able to trust people. So you get a company together with people you know are good, and you know work hard and you can make good stuff. That's kind of what I want to do.'

This all sounds really exciting and it will be great to see Rob with the ability to make movies exactly the way he wants them. He might even ask directors like Chris Weitz and fellow actors Jackson Rathbone and Kellan Lutz to become involved in his production company.

Smoking

Rob might seem like the perfect man, but some fans think his smoking habit lets him down. Quite a lot of actors smoke and Rob does, too. When enjoying meals with Kristen and the rest of the *Twilight Saga* cast, he often has to step outside the restaurant to have a cigarette. Some fans like being able to corner him when he's smoking outside and ask for photos and autographs, but the vast majority would love it if Rob stopped smoking. In a recent survey, 79 per cent of fans said they think both Rob and Kristen need to kick the habit, with only 21 per cent thinking it's okay that they smoke.

Because both Rob and Kristen have huge fan bases, many people believe they set a bad example to young people by smoking. Others are worried that Rob and Kristen are damaging their bodies and could have serious health problems when they get older if they don't stop smoking soon. No one is sure how many cigarettes Rob smokes a day, or if he just smokes socially on nights out, but no one would like to see his music career end before it's really begun if he damages his throat through smoking.

Stalkers

Every celebrity has stalkers but Rob seems to have more than most.

Rob's first stalker arrived on the scene in Italy when he was filming *Little Ashes* in 2008. Since then, lots of girls and women have become obsessed with him. The dictionary definition of a 'stalker' is a person who follows or observes someone persistently, especially out of obsession or derangement. Regular fans know where to draw the line.

Rob explained what happed to *Crème* magazine: 'I had a stalker while filming a movie in Spain last year. She stood outside of my apartment every day for weeks – all day, every day. I was so bored and lonely that I went out and had dinner with her. I just complained about everything in my life and she never came back. People get bored of me in, like, two minutes.'

Other stalkers have found out the location of Rob's LA apartment and have demanded he speaks to them. They have left notes on his car that start out friendly, asking him to call them, and then, as each day passes,

Rob likes meeting his fans but has to be careful if they cross the line into stalking.

they become more and more obsessive. One note said that a girl was going to kill herself if Rob didn't speak to her. It must have been hard for him to read that and even harder to decide what to do – he probably felt that he had to speak to her just in case she went through with her threat. It's definitely not all fun and games being a famous movie star.

It's awful that Rob is being pestered at home and it must be quite frightening to know that people will do anything to get close to you. On set, he has bodyguards to protect him but he doesn't have them with him at home. Rob tries not to let the fact that he has stalkers change the way he does things.

He confided in Collider.com: 'My brain doesn't really accept fame so it's fine. I can be put anywhere and it just goes completely over my head. I just don't want to get shot or stabbed. I don't want someone to have a needle and I'll get AIDS afterwards, that's my only real fear. Whenever I see a crowd, I always think that. It's like being on a plane: I think the bottom is going to hit the runway when it's taking off.'

Rob knows that he probably has a lot of stalkers who believe they are Bella and he is Edward, and they can't just see him as an actor playing a part. He told *SciFi*: 'I think that for a lot of fans of the book it's become a kind of cult now that they feel like defending. Other young people want to join it because they feel like they're missing out on something. I think it's a rolling stone gathering more and more people with it. I don't know for sure, I can't really tell you. What I always thought about it when I read the book was that it seemed like Stephenie Meyer completely believed that she was Bella and so in a lot of ways, when you're reading it, it seems uncomfortably voyeuristic, like you're reading somebody's fantasy. And after meeting Stephenie Meyer, it's absolutely not the case. But I really, really thought when I was going to meet Stephenie that it was going to be a very strange experience, with her thinking that I was a character. I think that's one of the reasons, that it's just such an intimate thing that people can really belong to. It's just one of these rare things that everybody wants to have a piece of.'

Poor Kristen Stewart has been receiving hate mail from some of Rob's stalkers because they're jealous of her friendship with him. They think they would be able to marry Rob, if she wasn't around.

In many ways, it's good that Rob is wary of stalkers as they could put his life at risk one day. So far he hasn't had to go to court to have a restraining order placed on anyone but other stars have had to take that drastic step to keep themselves and their families safe. In November 2009, Justin Timberlake got a restraining order against a stalker who broke into his home and said she was going to marry him. And Miley Cyrus has a stalker who is now in prison after sneaking on to her movie set, writing her love letters and claiming she sent him subliminal messages on TV. It's really scary and *Twilight* fans hope that Rob's bodyguards keep him safe.

Stephenie Meyer

Stephenie Meyer is the author of the *Twilight Saga*. On 2 June 2003, she was a housewife looking after her three sons when she had a dream about a young girl and a vampire. The next day, *Twilight* was born.

Stephenie says: 'Though I had a million things to do, I stayed in bed, thinking about the dream. Unwillingly, I eventually got up and did the immediate necessities, and then put everything that I possibly could on the back burner and sat down at the computer to write – something I hadn't done in so long that I wondered why I was bothering.'

Once she had put her sons to bed each night, she set about writing and it took her three months to complete. She never expected *Twilight* to be so successful as a book or that it would be a massive box-office smash a few years later.

Although she was over the moon when she learned that *Twilight* the movie was going to be made, she was gutted her perfect Edward, Henry Cavill, was too old to play the part as he was twenty-four. However, when told that Rob would play her hero after she had seen

STEPHENIE MEYER

him act, she gave him her full blessing. This helped turn the tide of the hate campaign demanding Rob be dropped: over 75,000 people signed a petition saying that there was no way he could play Edward.

Rob confessed to *The Big Issue*: 'People sent me hate mail and the Internet was full of messages from *Twilight* fans who didn't want me. They said I looked like a bum. My mother told me she had read online that I was wretched and ugly, and had the face of a gargoyle.'

Many gave him the benefit of the doubt once Stephenie said she thought he would do a good job. She explained to the *Los Angeles Times*: 'The thing is, he looks different when he does characters. When you watch the films that he's done, you might not be able to put [them] together with the same person because he's such a chameleon. There were times when he was just being Rob and then you'd hear "Action!" and he'd step into character – and he'd look different! He'd sound like Edward! It was crazy. He did such a good job.'

Rob and Stephenie have a really good relationship, but that didn't stop him from debating with Stephenie why the Edward Cullen in the movie needed to be different from the book's character. They spent hours discussing the matter but, in the end, they just had to agree to disagree.

He told goodprattle.com: 'I was talking to Stephenie Meyer, saying, "The guy must be chronically depressed," and she was saying, "No, he's not, he's not, he's not." But I still maintain he was. I mean, it's not like depressed, but just this sort of loneliness. I mean, when you see him at school, he doesn't really talk to anyone. He must get bored after a while only hanging out with the same four people in his life.'

The press reported this debate as if it had been a big argument and said that Rob and Stephenie had fallen out over the issue. This simply wasn't true. Stephenie decided to speak out and put the record straight: she did sit down with Rob to discuss Edward's character before filming for *Twilight* began, but they didn't fall out.

She told ReelzChannel: 'It wasn't an argument, but we [did] actually disagree on his character. I'd be like, "No, this is how it is." He's like, "No, it's definitely this way." Yet in the performance he did what he wanted, and yet it was exactly what I wanted.'

Rob had a challenge in trying to get his head around Edward's situation so it really helped being able to discuss things with Stephenie. He spent time thinking about whether Edward would have the mentality of a one-hundred-and-eight-year-old or a seventeen-year-old, as he himself had been seventeen when Carlisle turned him into a vampire.

Rob explained his feelings about Edward to goodprattle.com: 'You can have as many experiences as you want but, if you're still in the mind of a seventeen-year-old, it must be very frustrating; or having the world still see you as a kid when you're not a kid any more, things like that. I think that a lot of how people mature is just the rest of the world treating you like an older person, not just living a long time. Because he [Edward] knows he essentially is still seventeen, in most ways, and at the same time he's not.'

He also talked further on how he sees Edward to *Vanity Fair.* 'When his life is put into basic terms, he has nothing to live for and all he wants to do is either become a human or die. The only reason that he hasn't died is because he is too scared; he doesn't think that he has a soul. Then he meets Bella, who makes him feel like a human and feel alive again. At the same time, her human vulnerability makes him incredibly vulnerable,

EDWARD TAKES BELLA TO THE PROM.

because, even with his super speed and his super strength, he still can't fully protect her. Whenever she is in danger, he is in danger. If she dies or goes anywhere, then he is gone, too.'

Summer House, The

The film that Rob did after the made-for-TV movie *The Bad Mother's Handbook* was so small that you will hardly find any information on it anywhere. *The Summer House* (2008) was an independent British movie in which Rob plays the part of Richard, a grovelling boyfriend who cheats on his girlfriend and then has to follow her to France to try to win her back. Just 12 minutes long, it had a really low budget. It was made for film festivals and no DVD release has yet been confirmed but, hopefully, fans will get a chance to see Rob looking all tanned and gorgeous as he tries to woo the woman he loves. After this film, he went on to play Art in *How to Be*.

T is for...

Taylor Lautner

In the *Twilight Saga* movies, Taylor Lautner plays Jacob Black. After *New Moon* came out on 20 November 2009, quite a few fans moved from Team Edward to Team Jacob, but Rob's fan base is still larger. It's thought that Rob, Taylor and Zac Efron will eventually replace Brad Pitt, George Clooney and Hugh Grant in romantic comedy roles.

Edward and Jacob might hate each other, but Rob and Taylor get on really well. Rob admits that he would never challenge Taylor to a fight because of Taylor's martial-arts skills. He told journalists that he

Taylor Lautner as Jacob Black.

was really shocked when he saw the 'new' buff Taylor: 'I hadn't worked out at all until I saw Taylor at the beginning of the year. I felt incredibly inadequate and emasculated. I had a pre-pubscent teen body – I had A-cups! I needed to change that.'

Rob has even admitted to Taylor that he would love to play Jacob, if he wasn't playing Edward. He told him: 'I've always wanted your part – even when we're doing scenes together!'

But Taylor doesn't feel the same passion for Rob's character and he replied: 'Is Bella an option? I would love to get inside Bella's mind! A lot of weird things are going on in there – I would love to experience that.'

It's funny that Taylor wouldn't want to play Edward. Maybe he thinks that no one can play Edward better than Rob.

Teeth

When Rob first got the part of Edward Cullen, Catherine Hardwicke may have thought that he was the perfect Edward, but others weren't so convinced. *Twilight* producers didn't like his teeth and wanted him to have an operation on his gums before filming started.

Rob spilled the beans to a reporter from *B96*: 'Yeah, they tried to put a brace on me. I'll hold that against the people who decided that. The amount of stuff they wanted to do to my teeth – they wanted to give me gum surgery and put this, like, Invisalign thing [special plastic liners that are used to move teeth, like braces do] on and I was just [shocked face] and the producers were like, "How much is that going to cost?" and I was just listening, going, "Wwwwwwait, I'm not cutting all my gums off! What are you talking about?"

'I didn't, I just pretended. They did the whole Invisalign thing, the whole treatment. I wore it for maybe fifteen minutes and then I told the producers I was wearing it for a good month and a half before I had the guts to tell them. People were saying, "Your teeth look so much better" – it's the power of suggestion.'

Poor Rob!

Other famous actors and actresses reputed to have had work on their teeth for the perfect Hollywood smile include Tom Cruise, Nicolas Cage and Miley Cyrus.

Temptation

For its release in France on 18 November 2009, *New Moon* was renamed *Twilight Chapitre 2 – Tentation*. 'Tentation' translates as 'temptation'. That's a really clever title for the second *Twilight* movie because Bella is tempted throughout as she is drawn closer to Jacob.

During the French press conference, Rob was asked how he deals with temptation. With a laugh, he told journalists: 'I'm pretty good at resisting almost any form of temptation, to be honest. I have very few interests.'

Rob admires the way Edward resists the urge to kill Bella, even though he is forever tempted by her smell. Kristen admitted at the press conference: 'In my opinion, as much as they're always trying to control themselves and as much as the relationship is strained, if they were really denying themselves something, they would take themselves out of the situation completely; they wouldn't be with each other. They're willing to do literally anything, no matter how badly it hurts, to stay together. It is definitely a sexualised movie, it's just in a different way.'

Tiredness

Rob was asked during a *New Moon* interview whether he ever feels exhausted. He replied: 'It's weird because I'm dealing with two other films as well at the same time at various different stages of production and so I have so much adrenaline and, during these press things, I haven't been sleeping for weeks – it's a funny little situation to be in. I think maybe after the première of this I'm just going to collapse.'

He admits that he finds it hard to chill, but doesn't

feel the need to disappear to a remote island for a holiday, unlike many other young stars in his shoes.

These days, Christmas is pretty much the only time he gets to go home, but he must be so busy catching up with family and friends that he probably can't get much more sleep than he does while filming or promoting his movies.

Tokyo

Rob has visited some amazing places on promotional tours, but Tokyo has to be one of his favourites. It's one of the few places in the world where he can just blend into the crowd.

In a video interview, he revealed: 'I did go to Tokyo the other day, doing more press stuff, and no one recognised me and it was the first time in a year. It was amazing; it was absolutely incredible! I could go in fast-food restaurants and no one knows who you are.

'I was kinda shocked how apparently in Japan girls hate facial hair on Westerners, but they don't mind it on Japanese people. It's like really odd. They were very adamant that I had to be clean-shaven for all of the interviews.'

Toys

Rob was quite a shy child and liked to spend time on his own. His sisters enjoyed dressing him up as a girl and playing house. He has admitted: 'Up until I was twelve, my sisters used to dress me up as a girl and introduce me as "Claudia".'

Rob had a really happy childhood in Barnes with his mum, dad and sisters. This helped shape him into the nice guy he is today. He did lack toys, though. He told *Empire*: 'I didn't have very many toys – I just used to play with a pack of cards all the time. I'd pretend the cards were other things. I liked any toy that didn't involve playing with other children.'

Twilight

Robert never thought that *Twilight* would be as successful as it has been. If he'd known how much it would change his life, perhaps he might have thought twice about accepting the role.

He actually tried to read *Twilight* five months before his audition after someone recommended it to him but gave up after a few pages because he thought it was too girly. Months later, on reading the script he was impressed with the changes that had been made.

EDWARD AND BELLA IN *TWILIGHT*.

He told the *Examiner*: 'It cut out a lot of the descriptions… It read more like an action script. So, later, I went back to the book and saw what the differences had been. I looked at it a bit more objectively. I liked the book better when I came back to it the second time.'

Twilight was Rob's first American movie. When shooting began, he thought it was just another small-budget film and had no idea how huge it would get, not even while filming it. He only realised how big it was once the hysteria started, months after filming finished.

Robert actually put off going to the audition because he didn't see the point in auditioning. He thought the part would go to a model. As he explained to *Bliss*: 'I put off doing the audition for months because of that. I read the book and I thought, well, there is no point in going in. I thought that the whole point of the part was just to be a purely physical performance, like a modelling job. And I thought, I'm not going to go to the gym for one thing and so I'm already ruled out because he's meant to have this amazing body, too. I know they were casting for ages and I was one of the last people they saw.'

Filming *Twilight* was really enjoyable for him and he has many fond memories that he will treasure forever. He told *Vanity Fair*: 'I knew that there were some scenes where I was going to have to look demonic and have a glare that would scare humans. That was difficult to prepare. My favourite scene that we ended up shooting was this little random one near the beginning where I try and intimidate Bella by being a scary vampire and she doesn't back down at all.'

One of the trickiest scenes to shoot was the baseball one because Rob is rubbish at sports and had never played baseball before. Not only is Edward supposed to be able to play well, he's actually a great player. Catherine didn't want to change Edward's baseball ability so she had to get someone to teach Rob how to play – and fast.

'I'm terrible – I'm completely mal-coordinated, I'm terrible at all sports. Also, I don't see the point as well. I even had a baseball coach. Catherine was so determined to make me look like a professional baseball player and I literally couldn't take it seriously,' he told MoviesOnline.

Catherine was always honest with Rob and wasn't afraid to tell him when he was doing things wrong. In turn, he really admired her directing skills and the way she treated the cast and crew. He shared with the *Los Angeles Times*: 'She's such a free spirit! She has no filter – she kind of gets you out of nowhere. Like she'd go, "You know that thing you're doing there? Yeah, that. That's not good." And I'd go, "Really?" And she'd say, "Yeah, it's weird. And it's not working. At all." The diplomacy department is not her finest. But you love that about her, that she feels free to say, "That sucked. Try something subtler," which is really her way of saying *you* sucked.'

ROB AS EDWARD.

Twilight ended up being released a month earlier than originally planned after the *Harry Potter and the Half-Blood Prince* release was pushed back until July 2009 – leaving their original slot free. Summit Entertainment decided that 21 November 2008 would be the perfect time to unleash *Twilight* into cinemas.

Its main competitor at the box office was the Disney film *Bolt*, but *Twilight* well and truly trounced it from day one of its release. On the opening day, *Twilight* took an amazing $35.7 million at the box office – almost covering the whole costs involved with making the film. It was the 14th-biggest first day ever for a film and made Catherine Hardwicke the first female director to have generated such a large sum on a first day, too.

As more and more people went to see *Twilight* and reported back to their friends how good it was, the numbers going to see the film kept growing and growing. By the end of the first week, everyone involved in *Twilight* and movies in general was flabbergasted by its success.

Despite the fact that some magazine reviews claimed that *Twilight* was underwhelming and thought that Rob had struggled to pull off the role of Edward, millions flocked to the cinemas and left feeling it was the best film they'd ever seen. Quite a few had also been introduced to the man of their dreams for the first time.

Twilight fans criticised *Empire* for their review, which

claimed: 'Pattinson struggles at times – it's a demanding first lead role, requiring him to project a perennial restrained desire. He settles down eventually, but not before he's treated us to a series of hard-faced pouts.'

US magazine *Entertainment Weekly* became one of the biggest supporters of *Twilight* and said, 'Edward is Romeo, Heathcliff, James Dean and Brad Pitt all rolled into one... a scruffy, gorgeous bloodsucker pinup who is really an angelic protector.'

Before *Twilight* hit cinemas, Rob and Kristen had signed a contract saying they would play Edward and Bella in *New Moon* and *Eclipse*, but no one had any idea if they would ever be made. Catherine Hardwicke and Stephenie Meyer knew that *Twilight* would have to do exceptionally well for the other movies in the *Twilight Saga* to get the go-ahead and both were delighted when, only a few short weeks after *Twilight*'s première, Summit bosses confirmed that *New Moon* and *Eclipse* were to be made as soon as possible, with much bigger budgets than *Twilight* to ensure they were the best they could be.

U is for...

Unbound Captives

Rob will play the son of Rachel Weisz in the 1859 period drama *Unbound Captives*. He signed up for the movie as soon as he saw the script because he thought it was 'cool' and it reminded him of the movie *Giant* – one of his all-time favourite movies. In the movie, his father is killed and he is kidnapped by a Comanche war party along with his sibling. A frontiersman (played by *Wolverine* star Hugh Jackman) rescues his mother.

The film is to be directed by Madeleine Stowe – who wrote the script with her husband Brian Benben over ten years ago. Originally, she wanted to play the mother and had rejected a $5 million offer, but soon realised it would never be possible. Leading ladies need to be played by big stars to get people to go and see the movies. She decided to give Rachel Weisz the part instead.

Rob is excited about taking on a role that's the complete opposite of Edward Cullen: 'I'm playing a kid who is kidnapped by Comanches when he was four years old and he is brought up by them. His mother spends her entire life trying to find me and my sister. When she finds us, we can't remember who she is and can't remember anything about the Western culture she grew up in. I speak Comanche the whole movie. You can't really speak more differently from Edward.'

There is currently no release date for *Unbound Captives* as filming hasn't started yet.

University

By the time Rob finished his A-levels, he had had enough of studying and didn't want to go to university.

He explained his reasons to *The Times*: 'Even when I was 17 and I'd go to a student bar, I'd think, get me out of here! Not that I got accepted into any universities, not one.'

Rob isn't the only member of the *Twilight* cast to have snubbed further education. Kristen Stewart has no plans to go to uni for quite a few years yet and, if she does go, she plans to study in Australia. Maybe Rob will end up joining her there one day – but he won't be able to while the movie scripts keep rolling in. His fans would rather he kept acting than went to university, anyway.

V is for...

Vampires

Because Edward is a vampire, Rob was told to stay away from the sun and not get a tan. But this wasn't a problem for him. He told *You Magazine*: 'I don't like being in the sun anyway, which is pretty lucky. I'm English so I don't go there. I just go [laughter] red. I don't even go tanned. I guess you could have a red vampire, which makes a little bit of sense.'

Rob might have stayed out of the sun but he still wasn't pale enough to play Edward. He had to spend hours every day in make-up and hair to get his skin the right shade of glowing-white – he had to

SOMETIMES IT'S EASY TO FORGET EDWARD IS A DANGEROUS VAMPIRE.

look ghostly pale, along with the other Cullens in the movie.

Despite Rob not being comfortable with having his photo taken, he doesn't mind seeing his picture on the front cover of magazines because he thinks Edward deserves it. He believes Edward is a great character and should be admired.

He told Spanish *Glamour*: 'Edward is a vampire, he's not a hero like Superman – he's a vampire in love who wants to be normal. I've never been interested in vampires, although I understand why they're so appealing to some people.'

In many ways, Rob believes that Edward should have never become a vampire in the first place. He thinks that Carlisle Cullen should simply have let him die instead of turning him into a vampire. He shared with *MTV*: 'The way a vampire gets made is you just get bitten by someone. I mean, it's just like a disease. They're not separate entities to the rest of the world, they are much more human. You're just a human, you get bitten by another human who's been turned into this thing, and you just have to live forever afterwards. And you have these powers, you have super-strength and really amazing agility, but the pros for being a vampire don't really outweigh the cons at all. You can never reveal that you're a vampire, so you're just trapped in this kind of purgatory all the time. You can do a couple of cool things [laughs]. But it gets old after, like, 400 years. And also, you have to go around killing people all the time, which is another bummer.'

Rob can't understand why girls love vampires but Kristen Stewart knows why. She believes: 'It's because vampires are classically meant to draw you into the point where they have you in a complete submitting state to where they can kill you. So that's a little bit sexy, to completely let something take over. It's forbidden fruit. It's something you can't have, you just want more.'

Vanity Fair

Rob's first movie role was playing Reese Witherspoon's son in the 2004 movie *Vanity Fair*. He was shocked when he got the part because he had never been to drama school.

He expressed how it felt to MoviesOnline: 'You turn up on set and I'd done one amateur play, and you kind of end up doing a film with Reese Witherspoon and you have a trailer and stuff. It was the most ridiculous thing. And I was thinking, "I should be an actor. I'm doing a movie with Reese Witherspoon." How is this happening?'

He realised then that being an actor would be a cool full-time profession – it would allow him to express himself, something he couldn't do if he got a job in an office.

ROB IN *VANITY FAIR*.

'You get a lot of slack as an actor. You can just go nuts all the time,' he admitted.

We are so glad Rob decided to become an actor – he would have been wasted in any other profession.

Reese Witherspoon was recently asked what she thought of Rob before he became the big movie star we know and love. She said: 'I remember he was verrrrrry handsome! I was like, "I have a really handsome son!" I had to sob and cry all over him, but he was great.'

It was actually quite funny that Rob was picked to play Reese's son in the movie – he is only ten years younger than her.

Rob is actually rumoured to be working with Reese Witherspoon again in the near future. Reports suggest that he will star with Reese and Sean Penn in a movie called *Water for Elephants*. If they do sign up for the film, they will play lovers – what a difference a few years make!

Voice

Rob had to put on an American accent to play Edward but he found it pretty easy. His fans think this shows how talented he is as his accent is so convincing that no one would know he is English, not American.

Rob says: 'I didn't have a coach or anything. American's fine, but I've never really been a big one for accents. Whenever I try to do any accents, it ends up being a sort of Jamaican-Russian hybrid.'

When Rob plays Edward he finds it easier between takes if he doesn't go back to his British accent and instead stays in his American voice.

He told *MTV*: 'I do [stay in my American accent], kind of. For the big dialogue scenes, it's just easier to not keep switching between. I kind of do it by accident. I keep forgetting that I'm speaking in an American accent sometimes. The dangerous thing is that you end up forgetting what your real accent is after a while!'

W is for...

Werewolves

Taylor Lautner may think werewolves make better boyfriends than vampires because girls like to cuddle up to something warm at night, but Rob disagrees.

As he explained to one journalist: 'Well, vampires don't have to go around with a pack, I don't have to walk around with my shirt off all the time, like a dork. It's like driving a fancy car: "Are you insecure about something?"'

Working Out

Twilight director Catherine Hardwick believes that British boys tend to be like Rob and would rather be in the pub than in the gym. She thinks they are a lot different to American boys.

Rob agrees. He told *You Magazine*: 'I guess a lot of the British guys who come to LA get very much into the workout thing. There isn't really like a pub thing in LA; it's just a very different culture. I think people from LA don't really understand how it's such a normal thing to be in pubs from a very young age in London. People just think it's so strange, like drinking has such a stigma attached to it here. I have never really understood it – it seems so normal to me.'

Before filming for *Twilight* started, Rob did spend a lot of time in the gym, however, to try to get himself into shape because he felt a bit overweight. He had spent the year before chilling in his flat with his mates, eating a lot of pizza and junk food, and thought that he needed to get a trimmer figure so *Twilight* fans wouldn't be disappointed when they saw him. In fact, he ended up exercising too much and the *Twilight* producers were really shocked when they saw him.

He told *EW*: 'Three weeks before shooting the producers were like, "What are you doing? You look like an alien!" Oh, well, I thought it was a cool idea.'

Rob abandoned his strict exercise routine and soon began to look more like his normal self. 'I literally stopped exercising. Eating a cheeseburger after two and a half months of doing that – it tasted like ambrosia.'

Despite the fact that Kellan Lutz, Taylor Lautner and the rest of the *New Moon* actors love hitting the gym and all work out together, Rob doesn't join them very often. He just meets up with everyone when they've finished. They all enjoy going to watch Jackson Rathbone play with his band, 100 Monkeys, and catching a bite to eat together.

X is for...

X Factor

Rob loves watching the *X Factor* and *American Idol*. The *X Factor* judge Dannii Minogue has told him that he's welcome to come over for one of the live shows but it remains to be seen if Rob will make the trip from Los Angeles to London. He's just so busy at the moment so it would be hard for him to squeeze it in. Meanwhile, Rob's fans would love to see him given a bigger role and wonder if Simon Cowell would allow him to perform one of his tracks during the results show.

Y is for...

Youngblood

X-Men director Brett Ratner plans a big-screen adaptation of the superhero series *Youngblood* and he wants Rob to play the lead.

Youngblood tells the adventures of a team of superheroes who are employed by the government to fight supervillains. The leader of the superheroes is a former FBI agent who goes by the name Shaft. This is the perfect role for Rob.

Ratner told *MTV*: 'Definitely [Robert Pattinson] from *Twilight*. He just feels like he belongs in that world. I don't only see him as a vampire; he's a really good actor. [Pattinson] could do anything. He just has that look; I picture him on *Youngblood*, for sure.

'My vision for it is: we're going to make a very edgy, cool film. We're not soft-peddling it at all.'

Youngblood is set to be released in 2012 so it will be a while yet before the official cast list is announced.

Z is for...

Zac Efron

Just two years ago Zac Efron was the number-one heartthrob and the guy that every director wanted in their movie. Now things have changed and Rob is the actor everyone wants. Rob's fan base is a lot wider and he can play a whole variety of different roles, not just teen movies.

Despite this, Rob and Zac get on rather well and enjoy chatting to each other when they meet at the big awards shows. One day it would be nice if they could star alongside each other in a movie. Maybe Vanessa Hudgens and Kristen Stewart could become good friends too.

ZAC EFRON